MEALTIME MAGIC

What's easy but elegant, feather-light and delicious? The crêpe, of course—everybody's favorite dish and the most talked about cooking sensation in years.

Now you can explore a new world of gourmet cookery. Here's all you need to know about crêpe pans and techniques, together with 150 unique recipes from around the world.

Just follow the simplified directions to delightful dishes—appetizers, main courses, desserts—that bring tempting variety to all your meals.

CREATIVE CRÊPE COOKERY

by
WILLIAM I. KAUFMAN

PYRAMID BOOKS NEW YORK

CREATIVE CRÊPE COOKERY
A PYRAMID BOOK

Pyramid edition published September 1976

ISBN 0-515-04259-5

Library of Congress Catalog Card Number: 76-28158

Printed in the United States of America

Pyramid Books are published by Pyramid Publications (Harcourt Brace Jovanovich). Its trademarks, consisting of the word "Pyramid" and the portrayal of a pyramid, are registered in the United States Patent Office.

Pyramid Publications
(Harcourt Brace Jovanovich)
757 Third Avenue, New York, N.Y. 10017

CONTENTS

I

WHY CRÊPES?

ONE OF THE GREATEST JOYS of cooking—and eating, too—is rediscovering traditional foods that are both delicious and easy to prepare. Although a favorite with many cooks for generations, the crêpe has suddenly gained a new popularity. A star has been reborn, one that can play many roles: as an elegant main dish for lunches, brunches, and late suppers; as a tempting appetizer or a glamorous dessert for dinner parties.

Crêpes can be served in dozens of different ways—with meat or seafood, vegetables or fruit, to say nothing of the small bits of leftovers in your refrigerator which can be turned into delights when enclosed within a delicate crêpe and crowned with a perfectly seasoned sauce.

The recipes in this book, borrowed from kindly chefs throughout the world, will give you, I hope, ideas for an endless variety of ways to prepare and serve crêpes, whether for a quick little dinner for two or for an elegant and spectacular finale to a special dinner party.

THE PAN

One cannot produce a proper crêpe without a proper crêpe pan. But *which* crêpe pan to choose when confronted with the myriad varieties available becomes a problem without a bit of helpful guidance. Luckily, the very best pan is quite inexpensive so that you might consider buying two in different sizes; or two of the same size to speed the preparation of the crêpes. For instance, while spooning batter into one pan, you might be flipping the crêpe in the other pan; or while flipping one you could also be removing another, completed crêpe. (I would not advise attempting this juggling act on your maiden venture into crêpe-making, however!)

The traditional crêpe pan and, I believe, the very best is made of cast iron or heavy-gauge steel. It has shallow, sloping sides which meet the flat bottom of the pan with a definitive edge. The handle is angled so that the pan is easy to manipulate. The most useful size has a bottom diameter of 5½ inches and can be used for both dessert and entrée crêpes. If you are buying a French iron pan, this size will have the number 18 stamped on the handle. You may prefer a slightly larger pan for making entrée crêpes, perhaps one 7 inches in diameter. But remember, the best things are known to come in small packages, and that might well be true of the delectable morsel clothed in the thinnest of small crêpes.

Another excellent crêpe pan and a rather recent innovation is the so-called "dip-and-cook" pan. First you heat the pan, then dip it quickly into the crêpe batter. Turn the pan crêpe side up, place it over moderate heat for about 30 seconds, and the crêpe is done! The crêpe itself need not be turned. It is simply flipped off the domed surface of the pan onto the stack of completed crêpes. No excess batter clings to the pan so that each crêpe is a perfectly thin, delicate wrapper. The cooking surface of this type of pan makes a crêpe approximately 7 inches in diameter. If you decide to buy a dip-and-cook pan, make sure that it is made of heavy-duty metal. A lightweight crêpe pan, no matter what style, will not produce the best crêpes.

Other pans you can find on the market are made of aluminum, stainless steel, and enamel-coated steel or iron. There is even an electric crêpe pan—undoubtedly designed for the person who has everything! None of these, however, improves upon either the traditional crêpe pan or the dip-and-cook pan.

SEASONING THE PAN

Cast iron, heavy-gauge steel, and heavy-duty aluminum pans must all be seasoned before using. This is a simple process but requires several hours, so if you plan to make crêpes tomorrow, rush out today and buy your pan!

First, wash the pan in soapy water and scrub with cleanser or a scouring pad. Dry the pan and fill it with a ¼-inch layer of oil. Place the pan over moderate heat until the oil is very hot but not smoking. Remove the pan from the burner and leave the oil in the pan overnight. The next day pour the oil out of the pan and wipe off any excess with paper towels. Your pan is now ready to use.

If you have a dip-and-cook pan, after washing and scrubbing it, brush the cooking surface liberally with oil and heat the pan over moderate heat until it is very hot. Remove the pan from the heat and let it stand overnight before using.

Never, never allow anyone to use your crêpe pan for anything but making crêpes, and *never* wash the pan. After each use, just wipe it with paper towels and rub its surface with a thin film of oil. If bits of batter stick stubbornly to the pan, heat it, sprinkle a little salt onto the cooking surface, and after removing the pan from the heat, rub the salt vigorously over the spots with a paper towel. Wipe the pan clean with paper towels and rub with a thin film of oil. If your crêpe pan is inadvertently washed or put to a use other than crêpe-making, crêpe batter will stick to the pan and the pan will have to be reseasoned. Follow the seasoning steps outlined above, and this time hide the pan!

HOW TO MAKE A PERFECT CRÊPE

1. Make sure batter is the consistency of heavy cream. If it is not, thin it with a little milk.
2. Oil the crêpe pan with 1 teaspoon of oil.
3. Heat the crêpe pan over moderate heat until it is very hot.
4. Pour out any excess oil in the crêpe pan.
5. Spoon about 2 tablespoons of batter into the center of the pan and very quickly roll the batter around to coat the bottom of the pan evenly. Pour excess batter back into the bowl. (Remember, the crêpe should be paper-thin.)
6. Again, place the pan over moderate heat and cook the crêpe until it is dry and the bottom lightly browned. This should take not more than one minute.
7. Ease a flexible metal spatula under the center of the crêpe and turn it.
8. Cook on the second side about 30 seconds. (This side will not brown as beautifully as the first side. It will be the "inside" of the crêpe.)
9. Remove the crêpe from the pan. (You will have to throw away the first crêpe because it will have absorbed the excess oil in the pan.)
10. Stack the finished crêpes on a clean tea towel with the "insides" all facing the same direction.

NOTES ON MAKING PERFECT CRÊPES

1. If the batter forms a large lump or will not flow when you spoon it into the crêpe pan, your pan is too hot. To cool the pan just wave it back and forth in the air a few times.
2. If the completed crêpes seem to be getting thicker as you go along, the batter needs thinning with a little milk.
3. It is not necessary to separate the stacked crêpes with pieces of waxed paper. They will not stick together.

4. The thinner the crêpe the more delicately it must be handled. The first few times you make crêpes don't try to make them tissue-paper-thin. As you get the feel of the whole procedure, you will be able to make the thinnest possible crêpes with the greatest of ease.

FILLING AND SHAPING CRÊPES

The completed crêpes may be filled with an endless variety of savory or sweet morsels and may be heated with or without a sauce as your whims or the contents of your refrigerator dictate. Unfilled, they are folded into triangles and reheated in a sweet blend of liqueurs and fruit juices and, finally, flamed with Cognac to produce Crêpes Suzette.

Any filling you choose must be firm enough to hold its shape inside the very thinnest of crêpes. It is best, therefore, to add only enough sauce to the filling ingredients to bind them together. You can always put more of the sauce on top of the crêpes while they are reheating, or pass it separately when they are served.

Crêpes are usually filled and rolled into cylinders. But if you are filling them with something flat such as ham (spread with spicy mustard) or smoked salmon (spread with a thin layer of sour cream and sprinkled with dill weed), you can fold the filled crêpes in half and then fold the two sides in to form a pocket. Crêpes Suzette or any crêpes to be served without a filling are folded in half and then in half again to form triangles.

The recipes for fillings in this book show a yield of the number of *5-inch* crêpes they will make. If you are making 7-inch crêpes, you will, of course, allow more filling per crêpe and have fewer crêpes for the same amount of filling.

STORAGE

Completed, unfilled crêpes may be stored either in the refrigerator for two days or in the freezer for an indefinite period. They must be tightly wrapped or, preferably, enclosed in airtight plastic bags. If you freeze the crêpes, wrap them in stacks of four or eight, or whatever the number you will need to serve two, four, or even a crowd.

Filled crêpes will keep two days in the refrigerator if tightly covered with plastic wrap or aluminum foil. They may also be frozen in the pan in which you plan to reheat them. Or place the filled crêpes on baking sheets in the freezer and transfer them to plastic bags when they are solidly frozen. When reheating frozen crêpes, take them directly from the freezer and place them in a preheated oven. If filled crêpes are allowed to thaw out before reheating, they tend to become soggy.

REHEATING

Filled crêpes should be placed close together, or slightly overlapping if they are folded into pocket shapes, in a well-buttered, shallow baking pan. If you are not reheating them with a sauce, dot the surface of the crêpes with butter to keep them from drying out. Place the crêpes in a preheated 375°F. oven for about 15 minutes. It will take 20 to 25 minutes to reheat frozen crêpes. If the crêpes have been sprinkled with cheese or coated with a cheese sauce, you can run them under the broiler for a few seconds to brown the surface lightly.

SERVING

If you are serving crêpes for a light luncheon or dessert, you will need two for each person. As an entrée for dinner or supper, you should plan on three per person. (If your guests are especially hungry or if your crêpes turn out to be totally irresistible, you may need to have a few more filled crêpes ready to pop into the oven.)

Serve filled crêpes directly from the baking pan in which they were reheated if it is an attractive one. Otherwise, carefully transfer them to a serving dish or to individual plates.

Crêpes Suzette should always be served from the chafing dish or flambée pan in which they are prepared.

The ways in which you can serve crêpes are almost endless. Have you ever thought of having them instead of pancakes for breakfast? At a brunch for twelve (or more) you might consider making several fillings and letting each guest choose his favorite (or perhaps try them all). And then there is lunch, a prelude to an elegant dinner, a late supper after the theater and, always, there is dessert.

CRÊPE LEGENDS

It is believed that the crêpe originated as a special food to be eaten at the religious festival celebrating Candlemas Day, and down through the ages the crêpe has been associated with religious holidays and celebrations.

One of the most charming legends has to do with the invention of Crêpes Suzette. In 1897 the Comédie Française was presenting a play in which crêpes were served by one of the actresses, Mlle Suzette. The crêpes were made at a restaurant in the neighborhood of the theater, but by the time they reached the waiting mouths of the gourmet actors, they were cold and unappetizing. The actors threatened rebellion, and to stem the tide of discontent the ingenious chef created a flaming crêpe which he later perfected and named for the lovely young lady who had served them on stage.

II

BASIC CRÊPE BATTERS

BASIC CRÊPE BATTER

1 cup sifted all-purpose flour	1 cup milk
⅛ teaspoon salt	2 tablespoons butter, melted
2 eggs	

Sift together flour, salt, and sugar. Beat eggs and stir in milk and butter. Add to flour mixture and stir with a wire whisk until smooth. Or, place ingredients in blender or food processor and blend until smooth, stirring down any flour clinging to sides of jar. Place batter in a bowl and chill 1 hour. To cook crêpes see "How to make a Perfect Crepe."

Yield: 20 to 24 crêpes.

DESSERT CRÊPE BATTER

¾ cup sifted all-purpose flour	2 eggs
Pinch of salt	¾ cup milk
2 tablespoons sugar	2 tablespoons butter, melted

Follow method for Basic Crêpe Batter but sift sugar along with flour and salt. Dessert crêpes cook more rapidly than other crêpes because of the sugar in the

14

batter. Cook 25 to 30 seconds on first side and 15 to 20 seconds on second side.

Yield: 18 to 22 crêpes.

WHOLE-WHEAT CRÊPE BATTER

1 cup sifted whole-wheat pastry flour
¼ teaspoon salt
2 eggs

1¼ cups milk
1 tablespoon butter, melted

Follow method for Basic Crêpe Batter. More milk is required because whole-wheat flour absorbs more liquid than all-purpose flour.

Yield: 22 to 24 crêpes.

BUCKWHEAT CRÊPE BATTER

1 cup buckwheat flour
⅛ teaspoon salt
2 eggs

1 cup milk
2 tablespoons butter, melted

Follow method for Basic Crêpe Batter but do not sift flour and salt.

Yield: 20 to 24 crêpes.

BEER CRÊPE BATTER

1 cup sifted all-purpose flour
¼ teaspoon salt
2 eggs

1 cup light beer
2 tablespoons butter, melted

Follow method for Basic Crêpe Batter. If batter needs thinning, use additional beer. Beer crêpes will brown only lightly.

Yield: 18 to 22 crêpes.

HERBED CRÊPE BATTER

Add 2 tablespoons finely chopped fresh herbs or 1 tablespoon dried herbs to Basic Crêpe Batter.

APPETIZERS

SWISS CHEESE SNACKS

1½ cups cream-style
    cottage cheese
1 teaspoon Worces-
    tershire sauce
⅛ teaspoon Tabasco
1 teaspoon sharp
    mustard
1 tablespoon
    mayonnaise

2 onion slices
6 parsley sprigs
1 cup cubed Swiss
    cheese
18 pimiento-stuffed
    olives
18 crêpes

Put all ingredients except olives and crêpes in blender or food processor. Blend until smooth. Using a small spatula, spread an equal amount of filling over each crêpe; fold into triangles. Secure an olive to each crêpe with a fluted pick. Chill briefly before serving.

Yield: 18 5-inch crêpes.

PARTY CRÊPES

1 cup small-curd cottage
    cheese
¾ cup chopped prosci-
    utto, or cooked, lean
    ham

¼ cup chopped corni-
    chons or sour pickles
1 teaspoon finely
    chopped onion
18 crêpes

Combine all ingredients except crêpes. Using a small

spatula, spread an equal amount of filling over each crêpe; fold into triangles. Chill briefly before serving.

Yield: 18 5-inch crêpes.

PARTY CRÊPES WITH CAVIAR

1¼ cups sour cream
¼ cup heavy cream, whipped

1 tablespoon minced onion
12 crêpes
¼ cup red caviar

Blend together ½ cup sour cream, whipped cream, and onion. Using a small spatula, spread an equal amount of the mixture over each crêpe; fold into triangles. Spoon remaining sour cream on each crêpe and top with a teaspoon of the caviar. Serve immediately.

Yield: 12 5-inch crêpes.

BLUE CHEESE CRÊPES

1 package (8 ounces) cream cheese
¼ cup crumbled blue cheese
2 teaspoons finely chopped onion

1 small clove garlic, crushed
¼ teaspoon Worcestershire sauce
12 crêpes
Watercress or parsley sprigs for garnish

Beat cream cheese until light and fluffy. Beat in blue cheese, onion, garlic, and Worcestershire sauce. Spread each crêpe evenly with an equal amount of filling and roll up. Chill 30 minutes. Cut each crêpe into quarters and arrange on a chilled serving plate. Garnish with watercress or parsley sprigs and serve with cocktails.

Yield: 48 bite-sized appetizers.

HORS D'OEUVRE CRÊPES WITH SMOKED SALMON

1 package (8 ounces)
cream cheese
¼ cup sour cream
½ cup finely chopped
smoked salmon
1 tablespoon finely
chopped onion
2 tablespoons finely
chopped parsley
15 to 18 crêpes
Watercress or parsley
sprigs for garnish

Beat together cream cheese and sour cream until fluffy. Stir in smoked salmon, onion, and parsley. With a small spatula, spread each crêpe with an equal amount of filling. Roll up crêpes and chill. Cut each crêpe into thirds and place attractively on a chilled serving plate. Garnish with watercress or parsley sprigs.

Yield: 45 to 54 bite-sized appetizers.

CRÊPE ROLLS WITH SHRIMP

1 package (8 ounces)
cream cheese
¾ cup finely chopped
cooked shrimp
1 tablespoon finely
chopped onion
2 tablespoons finely
chopped parsley
¼ teaspoon dried thyme
¼ teaspoon dried
marjoram
1 teaspoon lemon juice
¼ teaspoon salt
Freshly ground black
pepper
12 to 15 herbed crêpes

Beat cream cheese until light and fluffy. Beat in remaining ingredients except crêpes. Using a small spatula, spread an equal amount of filling over each crêpe and roll up. Chill 30 minutes. Cut each crêpe into thirds or quarters before serving.

Yield: 36 to 45 bite-sized appetizers.

DEVILED HAM CRÊPES

3 cans (4½ ounces
  each) deviled ham
1 tablespoon finely
  chopped onion
2 teaspoons prepared
  mustard
1 cup sour cream
2 tablespoons finely
  chopped celery
2 tablespoons finely
  chopped parsley
12 plain crêpes
  Parsley sprig for garnish

Combine ham, onion, mustard, 2 tablespoons sour cream, celery, and parsley; mix well. Spoon an equal amount of the filling in the center of each crêpe and fold into pocket shapes. Place on individual serving plates. Top each with a generous tablespoon of remaining sour cream and garnish with a parsley sprig.

Yield: 12 5-inch crêpes.

CHICKEN TIDBITS

¼ cup mayonnaise
2 tablespoons finely
  chopped celery
2 teaspoons snipped
  chives
1 teaspoon Worcester-
  shire sauce
⅛ teaspoon Tabasco
¼ teaspoon dried basil
1¼ cups finely chopped
  cooked chicken
¼ cup diced pimiento
15 to 18 herbed crêpes

Combine all ingredients except crêpes. Using a small spatula, spread an equal amount of filling over each crêpe and roll up. Cut crosswise into thirds; secure each roll with a fluted pick. Chill briefly before serving.

Yield: 15 to 18 5-inch crêpes.

EGG SALAD BITES

¼ cup mayonnaise
¼ teaspoon salt
¼ teaspoon celery salt
⅛ teaspoon cayenne
¼ teaspoon paprika
½ teaspoon dry mustard
½ stalk celery, cut in
   2-inch pieces

4 hard-cooked eggs,
   quartered
12 crêpes
¾ cup sour cream
2 teaspoons prepared
   horseradish

Put all ingredients in blender except eggs, sour cream, horseradish, and crêpes. Add egg yolks. Blend on high speed one minute. Add egg whites. Blend on low speed just until whites are chopped. Using a small spatula, spread an equal amount of filling over each crêpe and fold into triangles. Chill briefly. Combine sour cream and horseradish. Place a spoonful of topping on each crêpe. Serve immediately.

Yield: 12 5-inch crêpes.

HAM AND CHEESE CRÊPES

1½ cups ground
   cooked ham
1 cup grated Swiss
   cheese
2 tablespoons chopped
   scallions
2 tablespoons chopped
   parsley

1½ cups White Sauce
   (see recipe)
Salt and pepper
   to taste
15 to 18 basic or herbed
   crêpes

Preheat oven to 375°F. Combine ham, ½ cup cheese, scallions, parsley and ¼ cup white sauce. Taste carefully for seasoning and add salt and pepper if necessary. Spoon an equal amount of the mixture in along one edge of each crêpe and roll up. Place close together, seam side down, in buttered shallow baking dish. Heat remaining white sauce and stir in remaining cheese. Pour over crêpes and place in preheated oven 15 minutes, until filling is piping hot.

Yield: 15 to 18 5-inch crêpes.

EGGPLANT TOMATO CRÊPE PIE

1 1-pound eggplant
Salt
4 tablespoons olive oil
1 or 2 tomatoes
15 to 19 whole-wheat crêpes

Freshly ground black pepper
Oregano
½ cup grated Swiss or Gruyère cheese

Trim off ends of eggplant. Slice crosswise into ¼-inch slices. Sprinkle both sides of eggplant slices with salt and place on a rack. Let stand 30 minutes. This will drain off the bitter juices. Dry eggplant with paper towels. Preheat oven to 375°F. Heat oil in a skillet and brown eggplant slices on both sides a few at a time. Drain on paper towels. Slice tomatoes thinly and remove seeds. Oil a shallow baking dish or cookie sheet. Place 3 crêpes on the baking dish. Top with an eggplant slice and a tomato slice. Sprinkle lightly with salt, pepper, and oregano. Top with 2 crêpes. Continue layering, placing 2 crêpes between each vegetable layer. Sprinkle the final layer of crêpes with cheese. Cover lightly with aluminum foil and place in the preheated oven 15 minutes. Remove foil and bake 5 minutes more. Run briefly under broiler to brown cheese. Transfer the crêpe pie to a heated serving platter with a spatula. Cut into wedges to serve.

This recipe is only a guideline. You can, obviously, make a pie of whatever height you or the quantity of your ingredients determine!

Yield: 6 appetizer servings.

IV
MAIN DISH CRÊPES

EASTERN SHORE CRÊPES

2 tablespoons butter
2 tablespoons chopped
  scallions or onion
⅓ cup finely chopped
  celery
¾ cup chopped
  mushrooms
1 can (7¾ ounces)
  crab meat, drained,
  rinsed, and flaked

2 tablespoons chopped
  parsley
¼ teaspoon dried thyme
1 egg, beaten
12 beer crêpes
1½ cups White Sauce
  (see recipe)
1 tablespoon sherry

Preheat oven to 375°F. Melt butter in saucepan. Add scallions and celery and cook until tender. Add mushrooms and toss over high heat 2 to 3 minutes. Remove from heat; stir in crab meat, parsley, thyme, and egg. Mix well. Spoon an equal amount of filling along one edge of each crêpe and roll up. Place close together, seam side down, in a shallow buttered baking dish. Combine sauce and sherry in saucepan; heat until it begins to simmer. Pour over crêpes. Bake in preheated oven 15 minutes.

Yield: 12 5-inch crêpes.

CRÊPES MICHELINE

3 tablespoons butter
3 tablespoons flour
1 cup light cream
¼ teaspoon salt
⅛ teaspoon pepper
¼ teaspoon minced garlic
1 teaspoon chopped
  parsley
¼ teaspoon dried basil
3 tablespoons tomato
  paste
2 cups cooked, flaked
  crab meat
15 beer crêpes
Watercress sprigs for
  garnish

Preheat oven to 375°F. Melt butter in saucepan; blend in flour. Gradually add cream and cook, stirring constantly, until mixture thickens and comes to a boil. Remove from heat; add salt, pepper, garlic, parsley, basil, and tomato paste. Add ⅓ cup sauce to crab meat. Spoon an equal amount of filling along one edge of each crêpe and roll up. Place close together, seam side down, in shallow buttered baking dish. Pour remaining sauce over crêpes. Bake in preheated oven 15 minutes. Garnish with watercress sprigs and serve.

Yield: 15 5-inch crêpes.

IMPERIAL CRAB CRÊPES

1 tablespoon finely
  chopped onion
1 teaspoon sharp
  prepared mustard
¼ cup mayonnaise
¼ teaspoon salt
⅛ teaspoon pepper
1 teaspoon lemon juice
¼ cup diced pimiento
2 cans (7¾ ounces)
  crab meat, drained
  and flaked
15 plain crêpes
½ cup grated Parmesan
  cheese
2 tablespoons butter

Preheat oven to 375°F. Combine all ingredients except crêpes, cheese, and butter. Spoon an equal amount of filling along one edge of each crêpe and roll up. Place close together, seam side down, in shallow buttered baking dish. Sprinkle with Parmesan cheese. Dot cheese with butter. Bake in preheated oven 15 minutes. Place briefly under the broiler to brown cheese before serving.

Yield: 15 5-inch crêpes.

SEVEN SEAS CRÊPES

1½ cups chopped cooked crab meat, shrimp or lobster
½ cup finely chopped celery
2 tablespoons finely chopped onion
1½ cups Seafood Sauce (see recipe) or 1½ cups White Sauce (see recipe)

2 tablespoons white wine or sherry
Salt and pepper to taste
15 plain crêpes
Watercress sprigs for garnish

Preheat oven to 375°F. Combine seafood, celery, and onion. Heat sauce and stir in wine or sherry. Taste carefully and add salt and pepper if necessary. Spoon an equal amount of filling along one edge of each crêpe and roll up. Place close together, seam side down, in shallow buttered baking dish. Pour remaining sauce over crêpes. Bake in preheated oven for 15 minutes. Garnish with watercress and serve.

Yield: 15 5-inch crêpes.

ORANGE CRAB CRÊPES

2 eggs
2 egg yolks
1 cup milk
1 tablespoon melted butter

3 tablespoons frozen orange juice concentrate
1 cup sifted all-purpose flour
½ teaspoon salt

Beat together eggs and egg yolks; stir in milk, butter, and orange juice concentrate. Add flour and salt; beat with a rotary beater until smooth. Or combine all ingredients in blender or food processor. Chill batter 1 hour, then follow recipe for Basic Crêpes.

Filling and Sauce

5 tablespoons butter
4 tablespoons flour
1 cup clam broth
1 cup milk
½ teaspoon salt
¾ cup cooked, chopped mushrooms
2 cans (7 ¾ ounces each) crab meat, drained, rinsed, and flaked

½ cup chopped toasted almonds
½ teaspoon dried dill weed
2 tablespoons frozen orange juice concentrate
2 teaspoons grated orange rind

Preheat oven to 375° F. Melt 4 tablespoons butter in saucepan; blend in flour and cook, stirring, 1 minute. Gradually add clam broth and milk to saucepan and cook, stirring constantly, until mixture thickens and comes to a boil. Taste and season with salt, if necessary. Remove from heat. Combine crab meat, mushrooms, almonds, and dill weed; stir in ½ cup of sauce. Spoon an equal amount of filling along one edge of each crêpe and roll up. Place close together, seam side down, in shallow, buttered baking dish. Add orange concentrate and rind to remaining sauce and pour over crêpes. Place in preheated oven 15 minutes. If desired, sprinkle with additional almonds. Serve immediately.

Yield: 18 5-inch crêpes.

ALMOND LOBSTER CRÊPES

2 tablespoons butter
¼ cup finely chopped
celery
¼ cup finely chopped
mushrooms
2 tablespoons finely
chopped onion
1¼ cups diced cooked
lobster
¼ cup diced pimiento

4 tablespoons dry white
wine or vermouth
1½ cups White Sauce
(see recipe)
Salt and freshly
ground pepper
12 plain crêpes
⅓ cup toasted slivered
almonds

Melt butter in saucepan; add celery, mushrooms, and onion. Cook until onions and celery are tender. Stir in lobster, pimiento, 2 tablespoons wine, and ¼ cup sauce. Taste carefully for seasoning and add salt and pepper if necessary. Spoon an equal amount of the filling along one edge of each crêpe and roll up. Place close together, seam side down, in shallow buttered baking dish. Combine remaining sauce and wine; pour over crêpes. Sprinkle with toasted almonds. Place in preheated oven 15 minutes.

Yield: 12 5-inch crêpes.

GOLDEN CRÊPES

2 cups chopped cooked
lobster, crab, or shrimp
2 eggs
2 tablespoons Cognac
2 tablespoons finely
chopped parsley
¼ teaspoon salt
Freshly ground black
pepper
15 to 18 plain crêpes

2 tablespoons milk
1 cup fine dry bread
crumbs
Oil for frying
Watercress or parsley
sprigs for garnish

Combine seafood with 1 egg, Cognac, parsley, salt, and pepper. Spoon an equal amount of filling in center of each crêpe and fold into pocket shapes. Beat remaining egg with milk. Dip each crêpe in egg mixture, then in bread crumbs. Heat oil to depth of ¼ inch in a large skillet. Fry crêpes, a few at a time, folded side down, for about 1 minute. Turn and fry 1 minute more. Drain on paper towels. Place on heated serving platter and garnish with watercress or parsley sprigs.

Yield: 15 to 18 5-inch crêpes.

NEW ENGLAND CRÊPES

1 can (8 ounces) oysters	½ teaspoon salt
Milk	Freshly ground black pepper
2 tablespoons butter	1½ cups chopped cooked
2 tablespoons chopped onion	lobster, crab, or shrimp
2 tablespoons diced green pepper	2 tablespoons finely chopped pimiento
3 tablespoons flour	18 crêpes
2 tablespoons sherry	Paprika

Drain oysters and reserve. Measure liquid from oysters and add milk to measure 1¼ cups; set aside. Preheat oven to 375° F. Melt butter in saucepan; add onion and green pepper and cook until tender. Add flour and cook, stirring, 1 minute. Add reserved liquid, stirring constantly until mixture comes to a boil and thickens. Stir in sherry, salt, and pepper. Chop oysters and combine with remaining seafood, pimiento, and ⅓ cup sauce. Spoon an equal amount of the filling along one edge of each crêpe and roll up. Place close together, seam side down, in a shallow buttered baking dish. Pour remaining sauce over top and sprinkle with paprika. Bake in preheated oven 15 minutes.

Yield: 18 5-inch crêpes.

CHINESE SHRIMP CRÊPE

2 tablespoons butter	¼ teaspoon Tabasco
2 tablespoons sliced scallions	1½ cups diced cooked shrimp
3 tablespoons flour	¼ cup sliced water chestnuts
1 cup clam broth	
⅓ cup light cream	12 to 15 beer crêpes
2 tablespoons sherry	¼ cup grated Parmesan cheese
½ teaspoon Worcestershire sauce	
	2 tablespoons butter

Preheat oven to 375° F. Melt butter in saucepan; add scallions and cook until softened. Add flour and cook, stirring, 1 minute. Add clam broth and light cream gradually, stirring constantly, until sauce comes to a boil and thickens. Stir in sherry, Worcestershire sauce, and Tabasco; heat. Combine ⅓ cup sauce with shrimp and water chestnuts. Spoon an equal amount of the filling along one edge of each crêpe and roll up. Place close together, seam side down, in a shallow buttered baking dish. Pour remaining sauce over top; sprinkle with Parmesan cheese and dot with butter. Bake in preheated oven 15 minutes. Place briefly under broiler to brown cheese.

Yield: 12 to 15 5-inch crêpes.

OYSTER CRÊPES

24 oysters or 2 cans (8 ounces each) oysters	3 tablespoons flour
	3 tablespoons sherry
	¼ cup chopped pimiento
Milk	2 tablespoons finely chopped parsley
2 tablespoons butter	
2 tablespoons finely chopped onion	Salt and freshly ground black pepper to taste
1 cup thinly sliced mushrooms	15 to 18 beer crêpes
	Paprika

Preheat oven to 375° F. Heat fresh oysters in their liquor just until edges begin to curl. Drain and reserve oysters and liquor. If canned oysters are used, simply drain them, reserving oysters and liquor. Add milk to oyster liquor to measure 1¼ cups; set aside. Melt butter in a saucepan. Add onion and cook until tender. Add mushrooms and cook over moderately high heat until liquid given up by mushrooms has evaporated.

Remove onion and mushrooms from saucepan with slotted spoon and set aside. Add flour to saucepan and cook, stirring, 1 minute. Add reserved liquid gradually, stirring constantly, until sauce comes to a boil and thickens. Stir in sherry, pimiento, and parsley. Taste carefully for seasoning and add salt and pepper if necessary. Cut oysters into ½-inch pieces and combine with mushrooms and ⅓ cup sauce. Spoon an equal amount of filling along one edge of each crêpe and roll up. Place close together, seam side down, in a buttered shallow baking pan. Pour remaining sauce over crêpes. Place in preheated oven 15 minutes. Sprinkle with paprika before serving.

Yield: 15 to 18 5-inch crêpes.

SALMON BROCCOLI CRÊPES

1 can (8 ounces) salmon	¼ cup diced pimiento
Milk	¼ teaspoon salt
3 tablespoons butter	Freshly ground black pepper
2 tablespoons chopped onion	1 cup cooked chopped broccoli
1 cup chopped mushrooms	18 beer crêpes
3 tablespoons flour	½ cup grated Swiss cheese

Preheat oven to 375° F. Drain salmon, reserving liquid. Remove skin and bones from salmon. Flake and place in a mixing bowl. Measure liquid and add enough milk to measure 1½ cups; reserve. Melt butter in saucepan; add onion and mushrooms and cook until tender. Add to salmon. Blend flour into butter remaining in the pan and cook, stirring, 1 minute. Gradually add milk mixture and cook, stirring constantly, until mixture thickens and comes to a boil. Remove from heat; add pimiento, salt and pepper. Combine ½ cup sauce with salmon, mushrooms, and broccoli. Spoon an equal amount of filling along one edge of each crêpe and roll up. Place close together, seam side down, in shallow buttered baking dish. Pour remaining sauce over top; sprinkle with cheese. Place in preheated oven 15 minutes. Run briefly under broiler to brown cheese before serving.

Yield: 18 5-inch crêpes.

CRÊPES ROMANOFF

1 can (8 ounces) salmon, drained
1 tablespoon finely chopped onion
¼ cup finely chopped green pepper
¾ cup small-curd cottage cheese
½ cup sour cream
1 teaspoon Worcestershire sauce
½ teaspoon salt
Freshly ground black pepper
12 to 15 beer crêpes
¾ cup grated Swiss cheese
Watercress sprigs for garnish

Preheat oven to 375° F. Flake salmon, removing skin and bones. Add onion, green pepper, cottage cheese, sour cream, Worcestershire sauce, salt, and pepper. Combine thoroughly. Place an equal amount of filling in center of each crêpe and fold into pocket shapes. Place slightly overlapping in a well-buttered shallow baking dish. Sprinkle evenly with cheese. Place in preheated oven 15 minutes. Run briefly under broiler to brown cheese. Garnish with watercress sprigs before serving.

Yield: 12 to 15 5-inch crêpes.

NORTH PACIFIC CRÊPES

1 can (16 ounces)
  salmon
  Milk
3 tablespoons butter
1 tablespoon chopped
  onion
3 tablespoons flour
¼ teaspoon salt
⅛ teaspoon pepper

⅛ teaspoon nutmeg
2 egg yolks, beaten
2 tablespoons grated
  Parmesan cheese
2 tablespoons sherry
15 beer or herbed crêpes
  Parsley sprigs for
  garnish

Preheat oven to 375° F. Drain salmon; measure liquid. Add enough milk to liquid to make 1½ cups; reserve. Flake salmon, removing skin and bones; reserve. Melt butter in saucepan; add onion and cook until tender. Blend in flour and cook, stirring, 1 minute. Add salt, pepper, and nutmeg. Gradually add reserved liquid and cook, stirring constantly, until mixture comes to a boil and thickens. Stir a little of the hot sauce into egg yolks; add yolk mixture to remaining sauce, stirring constantly. Add cheese and sherry and stir until cheese is melted. Mix ½ cup of sauce with salmon. Spoon an equal amount of filling along one edge of each crêpe and roll up. Place close together, seam side down, in shallow buttered baking dish. Pour remaining sauce over crêpes. Place in preheated oven 15 minutes. Garnish with parsley.

Yield: 15 5-inch crêpes.

SALMON MOUSSE CRÊPES

1 can (16 ounces)
salmon
½ small onion
1 3-inch dill pickle, cut
in 4 pieces
4 sprigs parsley
½ cup mayonnaise

½ teaspoon prepared
mustard
Juice of ½ lemon
¼ teaspoon salt
Freshly ground black
pepper
18 herbed crêpes
¾ cup sour cream
Dill sprigs for garnish

Drain salmon and remove skin and bones. Place salmon, onion, dill pickle, parsley, mayonnaise, mustard, lemon juice, salt, and pepper in blender or food processor. Blend until smooth. Spread an equal amount of filling on each crêpe and fold into triangles. Arrange crêpes on a serving platter and chill 30 minutes. Top each crêpe with a spoonful of sour cream and garnish platter with dill sprigs before serving.

Yield: 18 5-inch crêpes.

KING OF THE SEA CRÊPES

1½ cups cooked flaked
flounder or halibut
¼ cup seeded, chopped
cucumber, drained
½ cup finely chopped
celery

1 tablespoon capers
½ teaspoon dried dill
weed
¼ cup mayonnaise
18 plain or herbed crêpes

Preheat oven to 375° F. Combine all ingredients except crêpes. Spoon an equal amount of filling along one edge of each crêpe and roll up. Place close together, seam side down in shallow buttered baking dish. Pour Lobster Sauce over top. Bake in preheated oven 15 minutes.

Yield: 18 5-inch crêpes.

Lobster Sauce

2 tablespoons butter
2 tablespoons flour
½ cup heavy cream
½ cup chicken broth

¼ teaspoon salt
1 tablespoon sherry
1 cup finely chopped
  cooked lobster

Melt butter in saucepan; blend in flour and cook, stirring, 1 minute. Gradually add cream and broth and cook, stirring constantly, until mixture comes to a boil and thickens. Season with salt. Remove from heat; stir in sherry and lobster.

PORTSMOUTH CRÊPES

1¼ cups cooked flaked
  flounder
3 hard-cooked eggs,
  chopped
2 tablespoons chopped
  pimiento
2 tablespoons chopped
  green olives
1 tablespoon snipped
  chives

1½ cups White Sauce
  (see recipe) or 1½
  cups Seafood Sauce
  (see recipe)
2 tablespoons dry white
  wine or sherry
12 to 15 plain crêpes
2 tablespoons finely
  chopped parsley

Preheat oven to 375° F. Combine fish, eggs, pimiento, olives, and chives. Heat sauce and stir in wine or sherry. Add ⅓ cup sauce to fish mixture. Spoon an equal amount of the filling along one edge of each crêpe and roll up. Place close together, seam side down, in shallow buttered baking dish. Pour remaining sauce over crêpes. Place in preheated oven for 15 minutes. Sprinkle with parsley and serve.

Yield: 12 to 15 5-inch crêpes.

TUNA CRUNCH CRÊPES

1½ cups White Sauce (see recipe)

2 tablespoons dry white wine

¼ teaspoon ground ginger

1 can (6½ or 7 ounces) tuna, drained and flaked

½ cup sliced water chestnuts

¼ cup finely chopped celery

2 hard-cooked eggs, chopped

¼ cup diced pimiento

Salt and freshly ground black pepper to taste

15 to 18 crêpes

⅓ cup slivered toasted almonds

Preheat oven to 375° F. Blend together white sauce, wine, and ginger in saucepan; heat. Combine ⅓ cup sauce with tuna, water chestnuts, celery, egg, and pimiento. Taste for seasoning and add salt and pepper if necessary. Spoon an equal amount of the filling along one edge of each crêpe and roll up. Place close together, seam side down, in shallow buttered baking dish. Pour remaining sauce over crêpes; sprinkle with almonds. Bake in preheated oven 15 minutes.

Yield: 15 to 18 5-inch crêpes.

TUNA CRÊPES WITH CELERY SAUCE

1 can (6½ or 7 ounces) tuna, drained and flaked

¾ cup coarsely chopped cooked green beans

¼ cup chopped pimiento

2 tablespoons finely chopped onion

Few drops Tabasco sauce

Vegetable Sauce (see recipe), made with celery

Salt and freshly ground black pepper to taste

15 crêpes

⅔ cup grated Cheddar cheese

Preheat oven to 375° F. Combine tuna, green beans, pimiento, onion, Tabasco sauce and ⅓ cup vegetable sauce. Taste carefully for seasoning and add salt and pepper, if necessary. Spoon an equal amount of filling along one edge of each crêpe and roll up. Place close together, seam side down, in buttered shallow baking dish. Heat remaining sauce and pour over crêpes. Sprinkle with cheese and place in preheated oven 15 minutes. Run briefly under broiler to brown cheese before serving.

Yield: 15 5-inch crêpes

TUNA CHEESE CRÊPES

1½ cups White Sauce (see recipe)

1 teaspoon Worcestershire sauce

1 can (6½ or 7 ounces) tuna, drained and flaked

½ cup cooked peas and carrots

½ cup cooked chopped mushrooms

12 plain crêpes

½ cup shredded sharp cheddar cheese

Preheat oven to 375° F. Combine white sauce and Worcestershire sauce in saucepan; heat, stirring occasionally. Combine ⅓ cup sauce mixture with tuna and vegetables. Spoon an equal amount of the filling along one edge of each crêpe and roll up. Place close together, seam side down, in shallow buttered baking dish. Pour remaining sauce over crêpes; sprinkle evenly with cheese. Place in preheated oven 15 minutes. Run briefly under broiler to brown cheese.

Yield: 12 5-inch crêpes.

TARRAGON CHICKEN CRÊPES

2 tablespoons butter

¼ pound mushrooms, chopped

1½ cups finely chopped cooked chicken or turkey

1 tablespoon snipped chives

½ teaspoon dried tarragon

Salt and freshly ground black pepper

1 cup sour cream

12 herbed crêpes

2 tablespoons butter

2 tablespoons finely chopped parsley

Preheat oven to 375° F. Melt butter in saucepan;

add mushrooms and cook until liquid given off by mushrooms has evaporated. Stir in chicken, chives, tarragon, and salt and pepper to taste; heat. Blend in ¼ cup sour cream. Spoon an equal amount of the filling along one edge of each crêpe and roll up. Place close together, seam side down, in buttered shallow baking dish. Dot surface of crêpes with butter. Place in preheated oven 10 minutes. Spread remaining sour cream over crêpes and heat 5 more minutes. Sprinkle with parsley and serve.

Yield: 12 5-inch crêpes.

MATTERHORN CRÊPES

1½ cups finely chopped cooked chicken	¼ teaspoon sage
	Juice of ½ lemon
1 egg	12 thin slices Swiss cheese
¼ teaspoon salt	12 crêpes
Freshly ground black pepper	2 tablespoons butter
	¾ cup sour cream

Preheat oven to 375° F. Combine chicken, egg, salt, pepper, sage, and lemon juice. Place slice of cheese on inside each crêpe. Trim edges of cheese to fit. Spoon an equal amount of filling along one edge of each crêpe and roll up. Place close together, seam side down, in buttered shallow baking dish. Dot surface of crêpes with butter. Place in preheated oven 10 minutes. Spread a spoonful of sour cream on top of each crêpe and bake 5 minutes longer.

Yield: 12 5-inch crêpes.

HORNPIPE CHICKEN LIVER CRÊPES

3 tablespoons vegetable oil	3 tablespoons chopped mushrooms
1 pound chicken livers, washed and patted dry	3 tablespoons chopped parsley
5 tablespoons butter	½ teaspoon salt
¼ cup finely chopped onion	⅛ teaspoon pepper
1 cup white bread crumbs	15 to 18 herbed crêpes

Preheat oven to 375° F. Heat oil in skillet; add livers and cook, stirring, 5 minutes. Remove and drain on paper towels. Pour oil out of skillet. Add remaining ingredients, except crêpes, to skillet with 3 tablespoons butter. Cook, stirring occasionally, until bread crumbs are browned. Stir in chicken livers; remove from heat. Run mixture through food grinder using the fine blade. Spoon an equal amount of filling in the center of each crêpe and fold into pocket shapes. Place slightly overlapping in buttered shallow baking dish. Dot crêpes with remaining butter. Place in preheated oven 15 minutes.

Yield: 15 to 18 5-inch crêpes.

BACON AND CHICKEN LIVER CRÊPES

6 slices bacon	½ teaspoon salt
¼ cup finely chopped onion	Dash Tabasco sauce
	1 cup sour cream
1 cup thinly sliced mushrooms	15 herbed crêpes
	2 tablespoons butter
1 pound chicken livers, washed, dried and chopped	2 tablespoons finely chopped parsley

Preheat oven to 375° F. Fry bacon in skillet until crisp. Crumble and set aside. Add onion to skillet and cook until softened. Add mushrooms and cook over moderately high heat, stirring constantly, until liquid given up by mushrooms has evaporated. Remove onions and mushrooms from skillet with a slotted spoon and add to bacon. Add chicken livers to bacon fat remaining in skillet and cook, stirring constantly, 3 to 4 minutes or until done. Be careful not to overcook. Add chicken livers to mushroom mixture and stir in salt, Tabasco sauce, and ¼ cup sour cream. Spoon an equal amount of filling along one edge of each crêpe and roll up. Place close together, seam side down, in a buttered shallow baking dish. Dot surface of crêpes with butter. Place in preheated oven 10 minutes. Spread crêpes with remaining sour cream and cook 5 minutes longer. Sprinkle with parsley and serve.

Yield: 15 5-inch crêpes.

CURRY CRÊPES AU GRATIN

1½ cups finely chopped cooked chicken or veal
¼ cup finely chopped celery
¼ cup finely chopped toasted cashew nuts
2 hard-cooked eggs, finely chopped
¼ teaspoon salt
Freshly ground black pepper
½ teaspoon curry powder
¼ teaspoon coriander
1½ cups Curry Sauce (see recipe)
18 crêpes
½ cup grated Parmesan cheese
2 tablespoons butter

Preheat oven to 375° F. Combine chicken, celery, cashew nuts, eggs, salt, pepper, curry powder, coriander, and ⅓ cup curry sauce. Mix thoroughly. Spoon an equal amount of filling along one edge of each crêpe and roll up. Place close together, seam side down, in buttered shallow baking dish. Heat remaining curry sauce and pour over crêpes. Sprinkle with Parmesan cheese and dot with butter. Place in preheated oven 15 minutes. Run briefly under broiler to brown cheese and serve.

Yield: 18 5-inch crêpes.

CRÊPES LAFAYETTE

2 tablespoons butter
2 tablespoons flour
1⅓ cups light cream
¼ teaspoon salt
⅛ teaspoon white pepper
½ cup grated Parmesan cheese
1½ cups chopped cooked chicken
½ cup chopped cooked mushrooms
15 to 18 beer crêpes

Preheat oven to 375° F. Melt butter in saucepan;

add flour, and cook, stirring, 1 minute. Gradually add cream and cook, stirring constantly, until mixture thickens and comes to a boil. Season with salt and pepper. Remove from heat. Stir in ⅓ cup cheese. Combine ⅓ cup sauce with chicken and mushrooms. Spoon an equal amount of filling along one edge of each crêpe and roll up. Place close together, seam side down, in shallow buttered baking dish. Pour remaining sauce evenly over crêpes and sprinkle with remaining cheese. Dot cheese with butter. Place in preheated oven 15 minutes. Run crêpes under broiler to brown cheese lightly. Serve immediately.

Yield: 15 to 18 5-inch crêpes.

HONG KONG CRÊPES

1 cup cooked rice	2 tablespoons finely
1 cup minced cooked	chopped parsley
chicken or pork	1½ cups Bechamel Sauce
½ cup sliced bamboo	(see recipe)
shoots	2 teaspoons soy sauce
1 tablespoon minced	18 crêpes
onion	

Preheat oven to 375° F. Combine rice, chicken, bamboo shoots, onion, and parsley. Heat Bechamel sauce and stir in soy sauce. Add ⅓ cup sauce to chicken mixture. Spoon an equal amount of filling along one edge of each crêpe and roll up. Place close together, seam side down, in shallow buttered baking dish. Pour remaining sauce over crêpes. Place in preheated oven 15 minutes.

Yield: 18 5-inch crêpes.

HERBED CHICKEN MUSHROOM CRÊPES

2 tablespoons butter
⅓ cup finely chopped
   onion
1 cup thinly sliced
   mushrooms
2 cups finely chopped
   cooked chicken
¼ teaspoon salt

Freshly ground black
   pepper
1 teaspoon lemon juice
1½ cups Bechamel Sauce
   (see recipe)
¼ teaspoon dried basil
¼ teaspoon dried thyme
18 herbed crêpes

Preheat oven to 375° F. Melt butter in saucepan; add onion and cook until tender. Add mushrooms and cook over moderately high heat, stirring constantly, until liquid given up by mushrooms has evaporated. Add chicken, salt, pepper, and lemon juice. Combine sauce and herbs in saucepan; heat and add ⅓ cup sauce to chicken mixture. Spoon an equal amount of filling along one edge of each crêpe and roll up. Place close together, seam side down, in shallow buttered baking dish. Spread remaining sauce over crêpes. Bake in preheated oven 15 minutes.

Yield: 18 5-inch crêpes.

TURKEY CRÊPES WITH SPICY SAUCE

1½ cups finely chopped
   cooked turkey
½ cup finely chopped
   green pepper
¼ cup finely chopped
   pimiento-stuffed
   olives
¼ cup finely chopped
   onion
½ teaspoon salt

2 tablespoons Italian
   salad dressing
18 crêpes
1 can (8 ounces)
   Spanish-style tomato
   sauce
2 teaspoons minced
   green chili peppers
½ teaspoon chili powder

Preheat oven to 375° F. Combine turkey, ¼ cup green pepper, olives, 2 tablespoons onion, salt and salad dressing. Spoon an equal amount of filling along the edge of each crêpe and roll up. Place close together, seam side down, in shallow buttered baking dish.

In a saucepan combine remaining green pepper and onion with tomato sauce, chili peppers, and chili powder. Bring to simmer, stirring constantly, and pour over crêpes. Bake in preheated oven 15 minutes.

Yield: 18 5-inch crêpes.

ACAPULCO LUNCHEON CRÊPES

1 can (8 ounces) tomato sauce, or 1 cup Tomato Sauce (see recipe)
1 to 2 teaspoons chili powder
¾ pound ground beef
¼ cup chopped onion
½ teaspoon salt
1 cup grated cheddar cheese, divided
12 whole-wheat or buck-wheat crêpes
½ cup chopped ripe olives

Preheat oven to 375° F. Heat tomato sauce and chili powder in saucepan. Brown ground beef and onion in skillet, breaking up meat with a fork. Drain off accumulated fat. Stir in salt, ½ cup cheese, and ¼ cup tomato sauce. Spoon an equal amount of filling along one edge of each crêpe and roll up. Place close together, seam side down, in shallow buttered baking dish. Sprinkle with olives and pour remaining sauce over crêpes. Sprinkle with remaining cheese. Bake in preheated oven 15 minutes. Run briefly under broiler to brown cheese.

Yield: 12 5-inch crêpes.

MEAT-FILLED CRÊPES

2 cups finely chopped cooked beef, lamb, or veal
⅓ cup sour cream
Salt and pepper to taste
1 teaspoon Worcestershire sauce
1 tablespoon minced onion
2 tablespoons finely chopped parsley
15 to 18 plain or buck-wheat crêpes
2 tablespoons melted butter
Paprika

Preheat oven to 375° F. Combine all ingredients except crêpes, butter, and paprika. Spoon an equal amount of filling along one edge of each crêpe and roll up. Place close together, seam side down, in a shallow, well-buttered baking dish. Dot surface of crêpes with butter. Bake in preheated oven 15 minutes. To serve, sprinkle with paprika and pass additional sour cream separately, if desired.

Yield: 15 to 18 5-inch crêpes.

SOUTH AMERICAN CRÊPES

2 tablespoons olive oil
1 small onion, finely chopped
2 tomatoes peeled, seeded, and chopped
2 cups finely chopped cooked lamb or beef
¼ teaspoon salt
Freshly ground black pepper
2 tablespoons finely chopped parsley
18 buckwheat crêpes
1 cup grated mild Cheddar cheese

Preheat oven to 375° F. Heat oil in skillet and cook onion until lightly browned. Add tomatoes and cook, stirring occasionally, until mixture forms a mass. Stir in lamb or beef, salt, pepper, and parsley. Cook a minute or two until mixture is heated through. Taste carefully for seasoning. Spoon an equal amount of filling along one edge of each crêpe and roll up. Place crêpes close together, seam side down, in well-buttered, shallow baking dish. Sprinkle evenly with cheese. Place in preheated oven 15 minutes. Run crêpes under broiler to lightly brown cheese and serve.

Yield: 18 5-inch crêpes.

VEAL STUFFED CRÊPES

2 tablespoons butter
1 small onion, finely
   chopped
¾ cup thinly sliced
   mushrooms
1½ cups finely chopped
   cooked veal
1 can (4½ ounces)
   deviled ham
2 tablespoons sour
   cream

4 tablespoons finely
   chopped parsley
¾ teaspoon tarragon
   Salt and freshly
   ground black pepper
   to taste
18 plain or herbed
   crêpes
1½ cups White Sauce
   (see recipe)
   Juice of ½ lemon

Preheat oven to 375°F. Heat butter in a skillet and cook onion until softened. Add mushrooms and cook over moderately high heat, stirring constantly, until liquid given up by mushrooms has evaporated. Add veal, deviled ham, sour cream, 2 tablespoons parsley, ½ teaspoon tarragon, and salt and pepper to taste. Stir to combine ingredients. Remove from heat. Spoon an equal amount of filling along one edge of each crêpe and roll up. Place close together, seam side down, in buttered shallow baking pan. Heat white sauce and stir in remaining ¼ teaspoon tarragon and lemon juice. Pour sauce over crêpes. Place in preheated oven 15 minutes. Sprinkle with remaining parsley and serve.

Yield: 18 5-inch crêpes.

LAMB CURRY CRÊPES

3 tablespoons butter
¼ cup chopped onion
¼ cup chopped apple
1 to 2 teaspoons curry
   powder

1½ cups diced cooked
   lamb
1½ cups Curry Sauce
   (see recipe)
12 to 15 plain crêpes

Preheat oven to 375°F. Melt butter in a saucepan; add onion and apple and cook until onion is tender. Add curry powder and cook, stirring, 1 minute. Add lamb and ¼ cup curry sauce. Spoon an equal amount of the filling along one edge of each crêpe and roll up. Place close together, seam side down, in shallow buttered baking dish. Spread remaining curry sauce over crêpes. Place in preheated oven for 15 minutes. Pass a bowl of chutney separately.

Yield: 12 to 15 5-inch crêpes

ORIENTAL CRÊPES

1 tablespoon salad oil	1 tablespoon soy sauce
¼ cup chopped onion	1 egg, lightly beaten
¼ cup diced green pepper	18 plain crêpes
1 cup cooked diced pork	2 tablespoons butter
1 cup cooked rice	

Preheat oven to 375°F. Heat oil in saucepan; add onion and green pepper and cook until tender. Remove from heat; stir in pork, rice, and soy sauce. Add egg; mix well. Spoon an equal amount of filling along one edge of each crêpe and roll up. Place close together, seam side down, in shallow buttered baking dish. Dot surface of crêpes with butter. Bake in preheated oven 15 minutes. Serve with Sweet Sour Sauce.

Yield: 18 5-inch crêpes.

Sweet Sour Sauce

¼ cup firmly packed brown sugar	2 tablespoons soy sauce
1 tablespoon cornstarch	¼ cup tarragon vinegar
½ teaspoon ground ginger	¾ cup pineapple juice

Blend together brown sugar, cornstarch, and ginger in a saucepan. Stir in remaining ingredients. Cook, stirring constantly, until mixture is thickened and clear.

CHINESE CRÊPE ROLLS

2 tablespoons oil
¼ cup sliced scallions
1 clove garlic, crushed
¼ cup finely chopped
green pepper
½ cup finely chopped
mushrooms
¼ cup chopped water
chestnuts

1 cup chopped cooked
pork
¼ cup chopped cooked
shrimp
½ cup chicken broth
2 teaspoons soy sauce
1 tablespoon cornstarch
2 tablespoons dry sherry
12 crêpes
2 tablespoons butter

Preheat oven to 375°F. Heat oil in skillet and cook scallions, garlic, and green pepper until softened. Add mushrooms and cook, stirring, over high heat, until liquid given up by mushrooms evaporates. Stir in water chestnuts, pork, shrimp, broth, and soy sauce. Dissolve cornstarch in sherry. Bring mixture in skillet to a simmer and stir in cornstarch mixture to thicken sauce. Remove from heat. Place an equal amount of filling along one edge of each crêpe and roll up. Place close together, seam side down, in buttered, shallow baking dish. Dot surfaces of crêpes with butter and place in preheated oven 15 minutes.

Yield: 12 5-inch crêpes.

SPRINGTIME CRÊPE CASSEROLE

½ cup ground cooked
ham
1½ cups coarsely
chopped cooked
asparagus
⅔ cup grated Swiss
cheese
1½ cups White Sauce
(see recipe)

2 tablespoons chopped
pimiento
2 tablespoons chopped
parsley
2 tablespoons white
wine
18 crêpes

Preheat oven to 375°F. Combine ham, asparagus and cheese. Heat white sauce and stir in pimiento, parsley, and white wine. Add ¼ cup sauce to ham mixture. Spoon an equal amount of filling along one edge of each crêpe and roll up. Place close together, seam side down in shallow buttered baking dish. Spoon remaining sauce over crêpes. Bake in preheated oven 15 minutes. Serve at once.

Yield: 18 5-inch crêpes.

HAM A LA KING PANCAKES

1½ cups Béchamel Sauce (see recipe)
1 cup finely diced cooked ham
¾ cup cooked peas
¼ cup diced pimiento
15 crêpes
½ cup grated Swiss cheese

Preheat oven to 375°F. Combine ⅓ cup Béchamel sauce with ham, peas, and pimiento. Spoon an equal amount of filling along one edge of each crêpe and roll up. Place close together, seam side down, in shallow buttered baking dish. Stir cheese into remaining sauce and pour over crêpes. Bake in preheated oven 15 minutes. Run under broiler to brown cheese lightly.

Yield: 15 5-inch crêpes.

HAM SALAD CRÊPES

1½ cups ground cooked ham
⅓ cup finely chopped celery
2 tablespoons minced scallions
2 tablespoons chopped parsley
¼ teaspoon dried marjoram or thyme
¼ cup mayonnaise
¼ cup sour cream
2 teaspoons prepared mustard
15 to 18 herbed crêpes
2 tablespoons butter

Preheat oven to 375°F. Combine all ingredients except crêpes and butter; mix well. Spoon an equal amount of filling along one edge of each crêpe and roll up. Place close together, seam side down, in shallow buttered baking dish. Bake in preheated oven 15 minutes. If desired, serve with additional sour cream.

Yield: 15 to 18 5-inch crêpes.

HAM CRÊPES WITH SWEET AND SOUR SAUCE

1 cup finely chopped cooked ham	1 can (8 ounces) apricot halves
½ cup finely chopped green pepper	¾ cup chicken broth
1 cup cooked rice	1 tablespoon cornstarch
18 plain crêpes	1 tablespoon soy sauce
	2 tablespoons sugar
	2 tablespoons vinegar

Preheat oven to 375°F. Combine ham, ¼ cup green pepper, and rice. Spoon an equal amount of the filling along one edge of each crêpe and roll up. Place close together, seam side down, in shallow buttered baking dish. Drain apricots, cut into quarters, and reserve. Combine apricot syrup with chicken broth in saucepan. Add 2 tablespoons of the mixture to cornstarch and stir until cornstarch is dissolved. Set aside. Add sugar, vinegar, and soy sauce to broth mixture. Bring to a simmer. Add dissolved cornstarch and cook, stirring constantly, until mixture is thickened and clear. Stir in remaining green peppers and drained apricot halves. Pour over crêpes. Bake in preheated oven 15 minutes.

Yield: 18 5-inch crêpes.

CRÊPES MILANO

1½ cups grated Swiss or Mozzarella cheese	1 tablespoon snipped chives
½ cup cottage or ricotta cheese	15 herbed crêpes
½ cup finely chopped prosciutto or cooked ham	1 can (8 ounces) tomato sauce or 1 cup Tomato Sauce (see recipe)

Preheat oven to 375°F. Combine 1 cup Swiss cheese, cottage cheese, ham, and chives. Spoon an equal amount of filling in the center of each crêpe and fold into pocket shapes. Place slightly overlapping in shallow buttered baking dish. Heat tomato sauce and stir in remaining cheese. Pour over crêpes. Bake in preheated oven 15 minutes.

Yield: 15 5-inch crêpes.

HOT SALAD CRÊPES

1½ cups chopped cooked ham or tongue
¼ cup chopped pimiento-stuffed olives
½ cup chopped celery
2 tablespoons finely chopped onion
⅛ teaspoon pepper
½ cup mayonnaise
2 teaspoons sharp mustard
1 cup grated cheddar cheese
18 crêpes

Preheat oven to 375°F. Combine all ingredients except crêpes with ½ cup cheese. Spoon an equal amount of the filling along one edge of each crêpe and roll up. Place close together, seam side down, in shallow, well-buttered baking dish. Sprinkle remaining cheese over top. Bake in preheated oven 15 minutes. Run under broiler to brown cheese lightly.

Yield: 18 5-inch crêpes.

SAUSAGE SPINACH CRÊPES

2 tablespoons butter
1 tablespoon finely chopped onion
1½ cups chopped cooked spinach, very well drained
Salt and freshly ground black pepper to taste
12 plain crêpes
12 sausage links, cooked
1½ cups Béchamel Sauce (see recipe)
½ cup grated Cheddar cheese
Paprika

Preheat oven to 375°F. Melt butter in saucepan; add onion and cook until tender. Stir in spinach, heat. Season with salt and pepper. Using a small spatula, spread an equal amount of spinach over each crêpe; place sausage link in center. Roll up crêpes. Place close together, seam side down, in shallow buttered baking dish. Combine sauce and cheese in saucepan. Heat, stirring constantly, until cheese is melted. Pour over crêpes; sprinkle with paprika. Bake in preheated oven 15 minutes. Run under broiler to brown the sauce lightly.

Yield: 12 5-inch crêpes.

COUNTRY STYLE CRÊPES

½ pound bulk sausage meat
½ cup chopped onion
½ cup cream-style corn
¼ cup chopped parsley
12 whole-wheat crêpes
1 can (8 ounces) tomato sauce, or 1 cup Tomato Sauce (see recipe)
½ cup grated Swiss cheese

Preheat oven to 375°F. Combine sausage and onion in skillet. Place over medium heat, breaking up sausage with a fork. Cook 15 minutes, stirring occasionally. Drain off fat; stir in corn and parsley. Spoon an equal amount of filling in the center of each crêpe and fold into pocket shapes. Place slightly overlapping in shallow buttered baking dish. Heat tomato sauce and stir in cheese. Pour over crêpes. Bake in preheated oven 15 minutes.

Yield: 12 5-inch crêpes.

ITALIAN SAUSAGE AND TOMATO CRÊPES

1 tablespoon olive oil
1 medium onion, finely chopped
1 clove garlic, crushed
¾ pound sweet or hot Italian sausage
½ green pepper, finely chopped
½ teaspoon oregano
½ teaspoon basil
¼ teaspoon salt
Freshly ground black pepper
1 can (16 ounces) Italian style tomatoes
12 buckwheat crêpes
⅓ cup grated Parmesan cheese
2 tablespoons butter

Heat oil in skillet. Cook onion and garlic until softened. Remove sausage from casing and add to skillet, breaking up lumps with a fork. Cook over moderate heat 5 to 10 minutes, stirring occasionally. Add green pepper and cook 5 minutes. Stir in oregano, basil, salt, pepper, and 1 cup tomatoes. Bring to simmer, lower heat, and cook about 1 hour, adding remaining tomatoes as liquid evaporates. Mixture must be firm enough to hold its shape inside crêpes. Preheat oven to 375°F. Spoon an equal amount of filling along one edge of each crêpe and roll up. Place crêpes close together, seam side down, in a buttered shallow baking dish. Sprinkle with Parmesan cheese. Dot cheese with butter. Place in preheated oven 15 minutes. Run under broiler to brown cheese and serve.

Yield: 12 5-inch crêpes.

MEDITERRANEAN CRÊPES

1¼ cups diced Mozzarella cheese	15 to 18 herbed crêpes
½ cup ricotta or cottage cheese	1 cup Tomato Sauce (see recipe)
¼ cup grated Parmesan cheese	Parsley sprigs for garnish

Preheat oven to 375°F. Combine cheeses. Spoon an equal amount of filling in the center of each crêpe and fold into pocket shapes. Place slightly overlapping in shallow buttered baking dish. Pour tomato sauce over crêpes. Bake in preheated oven 15 minutes. Garnish with parsley sprigs and serve.

Yield: 15 to 18 herbed crêpes.

WELSH RAREBIT CRÊPES

18 beer crêpes
1½ tablespoons butter
1½ tablespoons flour
½ cup milk
½ cup beer
2 cups grated Cheddar
cheese
½ teaspoon salt
Freshly ground black
pepper
1½ teaspoons
Worcestershire sauce

Fold crêpes into triangles and place on a heated serving platter or on individual heated plates. In a chafing dish or saucepan, melt the butter. Add flour and cook, stirring, 1 minute. Add milk and beer gradually, stirring constantly, until mixture comes to a boil and thickens. Add remaining ingredients, stirring until cheese melts. Spoon rarebit over crêpes and serve immediately.

Yield: 18 5-inch crepes.

THREE CHEESE CRÊPES

1 cup small-curd
cottage cheese
½ cup grated sharp
Cheddar cheese
½ cup grated American
cheese
¼ cup finely chopped
pimicnto
1½ cups sour cream
Salt and freshly
ground black pepper
to taste
18 crêpes
2 tablespoons butter

Preheat oven to 375°F. Blend together cottage cheese, Cheddar cheese, American cheese, pimiento, and ¾ cup sour cream. Taste for seasoning and add salt and pepper if necessary. Spoon an equal amount of filling in the center of each crêpe and fold into pocket shapes. Place slightly overlapping in shallow buttered baking dish. Dot surface of crêpes with butter. Place in preheated oven 15 minutes. Top each crêpe with a spoonful of remaining sour cream before serving.

Yield: 18 5-inch crêpes.

NEAPOLITAN CHEESE CRÊPES

1 cup shredded Swiss or
Gruyère cheese
½ cup grated Romano
cheese
1 egg, beaten

¾ cup heavy cream
⅛ teaspoon white pepper
12 plain crêpes
½ cup grated Parmesan
cheese

Preheat oven to 375°F. Combine Swiss cheese, Romano cheese, egg, ¼ cup cream, and pepper. Spoon an equal amount of the filling in the center of each crêpe and fold into pocket shapes. Place slightly overlapping in shallow buttered baking dish. Whip remaining cream until stiff and spread over crêpes. Sprinkle evenly with Parmesan cheese. Bake in preheated oven 10 to 15 minutes. The cream will thin out and run slightly during baking. Run briefly under broiler to brown surface of crêpes. Serve immediately.

Yield: 12 5-inch crêpes.

SOUTH OF THE BORDER CRÊPES

2 tablespoons oil
¾ cup chopped onion
1½ cups grated Cheddar
or American cheese
12 buckwheat crêpes
1 cup Tomato Sauce
(see recipe) or 1 can

(8 ounces) tomato
sauce
1 to 2 teaspoons chili
powder
¼ teaspoon salt
Shredded lettuce

Preheat oven to 375°F. Heat oil in skillet; add onion and cook until tender. Combine ¼ cup onion and 1 cup cheese. Spoon an equal amount of the filling in the center of each crêpe and fold into pocket shapes. Place slightly overlapping in shallow buttered baking dish. Add tomato sauce, chili powder, and salt to remaining onion in skillet; bring to a simmer. Pour over crêpes and sprinkle evenly with remaining cheese. Bake in preheated oven 15 minutes. Run briefly under broiler to brown cheese. Garnish with shredded lettuce and serve.

Yield: 12 5-inch crêpes.

V

VEGETABLE CRÊPES

GARDEN CRÊPES

3 tablespoons butter
3 tablespoons flour
1 cup light cream
½ cup chicken broth
½ teaspoon salt
⅛ teaspoon Tabasco

1½ cups cooked mixed
vegetables
12 crêpes
½ cup grated Parmesan
cheese

Preheat oven to 375°F. Melt butter in saucepan; blend in flour and cook, stirring, 1 minute. Gradually add light cream and broth and cook, stirring constantly, until mixture comes to a boil and thickens. Season with salt and Tabasco. Remove from heat. Add ⅓ cup sauce to vegetables. Spoon an equal amount of filling along one edge of each crêpe and roll up. Place close together, seam side down, in shallow buttered baking dish. Pour remaining sauce over crêpes. Sprinkle with cheese and dot with butter. Bake in preheated oven 15 minutes. Run briefly under broiler to brown cheese and serve.

Yield: 12 5-inch crêpes.

ASPARAGUS CRÊPES
WITH HOLLANDAISE SAUCE

12 paper-thin ham slices
12 cooked asparagus
    spears
12 crêpes
 3 egg yolks

2 teaspoons lemon juice
½ teaspoon salt
¼ teaspoon paprika
¼ teaspoon dry mustard
½ cup butter, melted

Preheat oven to 375°F. Place a ham slice and asparagus spear in each crêpe and roll up. Place close together, seam side down, in shallow buttered baking dish. Place in preheated oven 10 minutes while preparing sauce. Put egg yolks, lemon juice, salt, paprika, and mustard in blender or food processor; blend 1 minute. Add hot butter in a thin stream while blender continues to run. Turn off machine when all butter has been added. Serve immediately with crêpes.
Yield: 12 5-inch crêpes.

ZUCCHINI CRÊPES WITH CHEESE SAUCE

2 tablespoons salad oil
3 cups coarsely
    chopped zucchini
¼ teaspoon salt
    Freshly ground
    black pepper
½ teaspoon dried
    oregano

1 tablespoon finely
    chopped parsley
18 crêpes
1½ cups White Sauce
    (see recipe)
½ cup shredded Swiss
    cheese

Preheat oven to 375°F. Heat oil in a skillet and cook zucchini, stirring constantly, until crisp-tender; stir in salt, pepper, oregano and parsley. Spoon an equal amount of filling along one edge of each crêpe and roll up. Place close together, seam side down, in shallow buttered baking dish. Heat white sauce. Add cheese and stir until cheese melts. Pour sauce over crêpes. Bake in preheated oven 15 minutes. Run briefly under broiler to brown surface of sauce and serve.

Yield: 18 5-inch crêpes.

SPINACH CRÊPES WITH CHEESE SAUCE

4 tablespoons butter
3 tablespoons flour
1½ cups half-and-half
½ teaspoon salt
¼ teaspoon white pepper
1 cup grated Swiss cheese
1 teaspoon prepared mustard
2 tablespoons finely chopped onion
2 cups cooked chopped spinach, well drained
⅛ teaspoon nutmeg
15 crêpes

Preheat oven to 375°F. Melt 3 tablespoons of the butter in saucepan; blend in flour and cook, stirring, 1 minute. Gradually add half-and-half and cook, stirring constantly, until mixture comes to a boil and thickens. Season with ¼ teaspoon salt and ⅛ teaspoon pepper. Reduce heat; add cheese and mustard, stir until cheese is melted. Keep warm. Melt remaining butter in saucepan; add onion and cook until tender. Add spinach and stir over high heat until excess moisture in spinach is evaporated. Season with nutmeg and remaining salt and pepper. Spoon an equal amount of filling along one edge of each crêpe and roll up. Place close together, seam side down, in shallow buttered baking dish. Pour cheese sauce over crêpes. Place in preheated oven 15 minutes. Run briefly under broiler to brown surface of sauce.

Yield: 15 5-inch crêpes.

ROMAN CRÊPES

2 packages (10 ounces each) frozen chopped spinach, cooked and drained
½ teaspoon salt
⅛ teaspoon white pepper
2 tablespoons melted butter
1 cup ricotta cheese
2 tablespoons heavy cream
1 egg, lightly beaten
½ cup grated Parmesan cheese
¼ teaspoon nutmeg
18 crêpes

Preheat oven to 375°F. Wrap spinach in corner of a

linen cloth and squeeze to remove moisture. Combine spinach, salt, pepper, and 1 tablespoon butter. Stir in ricotta, cream, egg, 2 tablespoons Parmesan cheese, and nutmeg; mix well. Spoon an equal amount of filling in center of each crêpe and fold into pocket shapes. Place slightly overlapping in a shallow buttered baking dish. Sprinkle with remaining Parmesan cheese and drizzle remaining butter over cheese. Bake in preheated oven 15 minutes. Run briefly under broiler to brown cheese and serve.

Yield: 18 5-inch crêpes

MUSHROOM SPINACH CRÊPES

2 tablespoons butter	⅓ cup whipped cream cheese
2 tablespoons finely chopped onion	12 crêpes
1 cup chopped mushrooms	1½ cups Béchamel Sauce (see recipe)
1 cup chopped cooked spinach, well drained	¼ cup shredded Swiss cheese
½ teaspoon salt	1 tablespoon white wine
Freshly ground black pepper	

Preheat oven to 375°F. Melt butter in saucepan. Add onion and cook until tender. Add mushrooms and cook, stirring, over moderately high heat until liquid given up by the mushrooms has evaporated. Add spinach and continue to stir until any excess moisture in spinach has evaporated. Add salt, pepper, and cream cheese. Spoon an equal amount of filling along one edge of each crêpe and roll up. Place close together, seam side down, in shallow buttered baking dish. Heat Béchamel sauce and add Swiss cheese and wine; stir until cheese is melted. Pour sauce over crêpes. Bake in preheated oven 15 minutes. Run briefly under broiler to brown surface of sauce and serve.

Yield: 12 5-inch crêpes.

CRÊPES A LA RUSSE

½ cup minced pickled
  beets, well drained
½ cup finely chopped
  cabbage
½ cup finely chopped
  celery
½ cup finely chopped
  green pepper

1 tablespoon grated
  onion
1 cup sour cream
Salt and freshly ground
  black pepper
15 crêpes
 2 tablespoons butter

Preheat oven to 375°F. Combine beets, cabbage, celery, green pepper, and onion with ⅓ cup sour cream. Season to taste with salt and pepper. Spoon an equal amount of filling along one edge of each crêpe and roll up. Place close together, seam side down, in a shallow buttered baking dish. Dot surface of crêpes with butter. Place in preheated oven 15 minutes until filling is piping hot but vegetables are still crisp. To serve, top with remaining cold sour cream.

Yield: 15 5-inch crêpes.

GARDEN PATCH CRÊPES

1 tablespoon butter
2 tablespoons chopped
  onion
1 cup chopped cooked
  broccoli
1 tomato, peeled,
  seeded, and diced
¼ teaspoon dried basil

½ teaspoon salt
Freshly ground black
  pepper
1½ cups shredded
  American or mild
  Cheddar cheese
12 crêpes

Preheat oven to 375°F. Melt butter in saucepan; add onion and cook until tender. Add broccoli, tomato, basil, salt and pepper, stirring until vegetables are heated through. Remove from heat; stir in ½ cup cheese. Spoon an equal amount of the filling along one edge of each crêpe and roll up. Place close together, seam side down, in shallow buttered baking dish.

Sprinkle remaining cheese over crêpes. Place in pre-heated oven 15 minutes. Run briefly under broiler to brown cheese and serve.

Yield: 12 5-inch crêpes.

CREOLE CRÊPES WITH OLIVE STUFFING

2 tablespoons butter	¼ teaspoon salt
⅓ cup chopped onion	Freshly ground
½ cup diced celery	black pepper
1 cup cooked rice	¼ teaspoon dried thyme
½ cup chopped pimiento-stuffed olives	15 crêpes

Preheat oven to 375°F. Melt butter in saucepan; add onion and celery and cook until tender. Remove from heat; stir in remaining ingredients. Spoon an equal amount of filling along one edge of each crêpe and roll up. Place close together, seam side down, in shallow buttered baking dish. Pour Creole Sauce over crêpes. Bake in preheated oven 15 minutes.

Yield: 15 5-inch crêpes.

Creole Sauce

2 tablespoons butter	1 can (16 ounces)
¼ cup finely chopped onion	Italian style tomatoes
	¼ teaspoon Tabasco
¼ cup finely chopped green pepper	½ teaspoon salt
	1 teaspoon sugar

Melt butter in saucepan; add onion and green pepper and cook until tender. Add remaining ingredients; simmer, uncovered, over low heat 30 minutes, stirring occasionally.

AVOCADO CRÊPES

1½ cups finely chopped
  avocado
1 medium tomato,
  peeled, seeded, and
  chopped
2 tablespoons finely
  chopped onion

½ teaspoon salt
⅛ teaspoon Tabasco
1 to 2 teaspoons curry
  powder
12 crêpes
Lemon wedges

Mash avocado with the back of a fork or blend until smooth in a blender or food processor. Drain chopped tomato thoroughly and add to avocado. Stir in onion, salt, Tabasco, and curry powder. Chill at least 30 minutes. Spread a thin layer of filling on each crêpe and fold into triangles. Top each crêpe with a spoonful of remaining filling. Serve garnished with lemon wedges.

Yield: 12 5-inch crêpes.

CRISPY BEAN CRÊPES

2 tablespoons oil
1 medium onion,
  thinly sliced
1 clove garlic, crushed
½ cup thinly sliced
  mushrooms

1½ cups green beans, cut
  into 1-inch pieces
1 teaspoon soy sauce
1½ cups Béchamel Sauce
  (see recipe)
12 crêpes

Preheat oven to 375°F. Heat oil in a skillet until very hot. Add onion and garlic and cook, stirring, until onion is transparent. Add mushrooms and green beans and continue to cook over high heat, stirring constantly, just until beans are crisp tender. Do not overcook. Stir in soy sauce and ⅓ cup Béchamel sauce. Place an equal amount of filling along one edge of each crêpe and roll up. Place close together, seam side down, in buttered shallow baking dish. Place in preheated oven 15 minutes. Serve immediately.

Yield: 12 5-inch crêpes.

REFRIED BEAN CRÊPES

1 can (20 ounces) red
kidney beans, drained
2 teaspoons chopped
green chilies
1 medium onion,
quartered
1 clove garlic
2 tablespoons oil
½ teaspoon salt

18 crêpes
2 cans (8 ounces each)
Spanish-style
tomato sauce, or 2
cups Tomato Sauce
(see recipe)
1 cup grated Cheddar
cheese

Preheat oven to 375°F. Put kidney beans, chilies, onion, garlic, oil, and salt in blender or food processor. Blend until smooth. Spoon an equal amount of filling in the center of each crêpe and fold into pocket shapes. Place slightly overlapping in shallow buttered baking dish. Heat sauce and pour over crêpes; sprinkle with cheese. Bake in preheated oven 15 minutes. Run briefly under broiler to brown cheese and serve.

Yield: 18 5-inch crêpes.

CHILI CORN CRÊPES

1 tablespoon oil
¼ cup finely chopped
onion
2 cups homemade chili
(in a pinch, use a 16-
ounce can)

½ cup whole-kernel corn
18 buckwheat or whole-
wheat crêpes
1 cup grated Monterey
Jack or mild
Cheddar cheese

Heat oil in a saucepan and cook onion until softened. Stir in chili and corn and bring to simmer. Reduce heat, cover, and simmer 20 minutes. Preheat oven to 375°F. Place an equal amount of filling along one edge of each crêpe and roll up. Place close together, seam side down, in buttered shallow baking dish. Sprinkle evenly with cheese. Place in preheated oven 15 minutes. Run briefly under broiler to brown cheese and serve.

Yield: 18 5-inch crêpes.

VI

DESSERTS

FRESH APPLE CRÊPES

¾ cup sifted all-purpose
flour
¼ teaspoon salt
⅛ teaspoon cinnamon
3 eggs
1 cup milk
3 tablespoons butter or
margarine, melted
¾ cup water
¾ cup sugar

3 cups pared and sliced
cooking apples
1 package (3 ounces)
cream cheese, softened
½ cup grated sharp
Cheddar cheese
½ cup sour cream
Butter, margarine, or
oil for cooking

Combine flour, salt, and cinnamon; beat in eggs, milk, and melted butter until smooth. Or place ingredients in a blender or food processor and blend until smooth. To cook crêpes see "How to Make a Perfect Crêpe." Combine water and sugar in saucepan. Place over low heat and stir until sugar is dissolved. Add apple slices and simmer until just tender. Reserve. Combine cream cheese and Cheddar cheese and beat until blended. Stir in sour cream; mix well. Reserve. Place 3 to 5 apple slices in center of each crêpe and fold into pocket shapes. Place seam side down in chafing dish. Pour in apple cooking syrup and any remaining apple slices. Baste crêpes with sauce. Serve crêpes topped with a spoonful of cheese mixture.

Yield: 18 5-inch crêpes.

APPLESAUCE CRÊPES

¼ teaspoon cinnamon
¼ teaspoon nutmeg
1 tablespoon butter
1½ cups applesauce
½ teaspoon cinnamon

1 tablespoon applejack
(optional)
½ cup heavy cream,
whipped with
1 tablespoon sugar and
1 teaspoon vanilla

Prepare a basic crêpe batter, adding cinnamon and nutmeg. Cook 12 crêpes following instructions in "How to Make a Perfect Crêpe."

Melt butter in a saucepan. Add applesauce and cinnamon, stirring until very hot. Spread each crêpe with approximately 1 tablespoon applesauce and fold into triangles. Arrange attractively on a heated serving plate and keep warm. Stir optional applejack into remaining applesauce and spoon over crêpes. Serve immediately and pass sweetened whipped cream separately.

Yield: 12 5-inch crêpes.

APPLE RAISIN CRÊPES

¾ cup seedless raisins
¾ cup chopped tart
apples
3 tablespoons butter,
softened
½ cup honey

2 teaspoons lemon juice
Grated rind of ½
lemon
¼ teaspoon nutmeg
12 dessert crêpes
¾ cup sour cream

Preheat oven to 375°F. Cover raisins with boiling water and let stand 5 minutes. Drain raisins and combine with apple. Beat butter and ¼ cup honey together until thoroughly combined. Beat in lemon juice, lemon rind, and nutmeg. Combine honey butter with raisins and apples. Spoon an equal amount of filling along one edge of each crêpe and roll up. Place crêpes close together, seam side down, in a well-buttered shallow baking pan. Dot surface of crêpes with butter. Place in preheated oven 15 minutes. Meanwhile, combine remaining honey and sour cream. Top each crêpe with a spoonful of sour cream and serve immediately.

Yield: 12 5-inch crêpes.

HAITIAN CRÊPES

1¼ cups prepared
mincemeat
1¼ cups finely chopped
apples
½ teaspoon salt

Juice and grated rind
of 1 lime
18 dessert crêpes
2 tablespoons butter

Preheat oven to 375°F. Combine mincemeat, apples, salt, lime juice, and rind. Spoon an equal amount of filling along one edge of each crêpe and roll up. Place close together, seam side down, in a shallow baking dish. Dot surfaces of crêpes with butter. Place in preheated oven 15 minutes until filling is piping hot. Serve with Haitian Sauce.

Haitian Sauce

1 tablespoon cornstarch
⅓ cup sugar
⅛ teaspoon salt
½ cup water
1 egg yolk
1½ teaspoons butter

Juice and grated rind
of ½ lime
1 tablespoon rum
1 egg white, stiffly
beaten

Combine cornstarch, sugar, and salt in saucepan; stir in water. Cook until thick, stirring constantly. Gradually add mixture to beaten egg yolk. Return to saucepan and cook 2 minutes longer, stirring constantly. Do not allow sauce to boil or egg yolk will curdle. Remove from heat; add butter and cool. Cover with wax paper and chill. Just before serving add lime juice, rind, and rum; fold in beaten egg white.

Yield: 18 5-inch crêpes.

SARASOTA CRÊPES

3 eggs
2 egg yolks
⅔ cup milk
½ cup orange juice
1 cup sifted all-purpose
  flour

⅛ teaspoon salt
1 tablespoon sugar
2 tablespoons butter,
  melted
1 teaspoon grated
  orange rind

Beat eggs and egg yolks together. Stir in milk and orange juice. Sift together the flour, sugar, and salt. Add flour mixture and orange rind to liquid ingredients; beat until smooth. Or combine ingredients in a blender or food processor and blend until smooth. Chill 1 hour. To cook crêpes see "How to Make a Perfect Crêpe."

Orange Sauce

½ cup softened butter
½ cup confectioners'
  sugar
1 tablespoon grated
  orange rind

3 tablespoons Cointreau
⅓ cup orange juice
1 cup orange sections

Beat together butter, sugar, and orange rind until light and fluffy. Blend in Cointreau. Using a small spatula, spread about 1 teaspoon mixture over each crêpe; fold into triangles. Place remaining orange butter with orange juice in chafing dish; heat. Arrange crêpes, slightly overlapping in chafing dish. Add orange sections and baste with sauce. Serve immediately.

Yield: 12 5-inch crêpes.

ORANGE COCONUT CRÊPES

For the Crêpes:

1 cup sifted cake flour
¼ teaspoon salt
2 tablespoons sugar
1 egg
1¼ cups milk

2 tablespoons coconut
Grated rind of ½
  orange
2 tablespoons butter,
  melted

Sift together the flour, salt, and sugar. Beat the egg

lightly and stir in milk. Add milk mixture, coconut, orange rind, and butter to flour mixture and beat until batter is smooth. Or combine all ingredients in a blender or food processor and blend until smooth. To cook crêpes see "How to Make a Perfect Crêpe." Cover 12 crêpes with foil and keep warm in an oven turned to the lowest possible setting. Or reheat crêpes in a stack in a 350°F. oven 5 to 10 minutes.

Filling:

1 package (8 ounces) cream cheese	1½ tablespoons orange juice
2 tablespoons sugar	Grated rind of ½ orange
¼ cup coconut	⅛ teaspoon salt

Beat cream cheese and sugar until light and fluffy. Beat in coconut, orange juice, orange rind, and salt. Chill in refrigerator while preparing sauce.

Sauce:

¼ cup sugar	2 tablespoons coconut
2 teaspoons cornstarch	1 tablespoon orange liqueur
⅛ teaspoon salt	
¾ cup orange juice	1 tablespoon butter

Combine sugar, cornstarch, salt, and orange juice in a saucepan. Cook, stirring, until sauce thickens and is clear. Stir in coconut, orange liqueur, and butter.

To assemble crêpes, spoon an equal amount of chilled filling into center of each crêpe and fold into pocket shapes. Place on individual serving plates. Spoon hot sauce over each crêpe and serve immediately.

Yield: 12 5-inch crêpes.

CRÊPES IN ORANGE TOFFEE SAUCE

12 to 15 dessert crêpes	2 tablespoons butter
2 eggs, lightly beaten	3 tablespoons orange juice
⅔ cup maple-blended syrup	Grated rind of 1 orange

Fold crêpes into triangles and place on a heated serving platter or individual heated plates. Place remaining ingredients in a double boiler. Cook, stirring constantly, until mixture thickens slightly. Do not allow sauce to boil or eggs will curdle. Spoon sauce over crêpes and serve immediately.

Yield: 12 to 15 5-inch crêpes.

CRÊPES WITH MOLASSES ORANGE SAUCE

12 to 15 crêpes	⅓ cup orange juice
½ cup dark molasses	½ teaspoon rum extract,
¼ cup sugar	or 2 tablespoons dark
¼ cup butter	rum

Fold crêpes into triangles and arrange on a heated serving platter. Combine molasses, sugar, butter, and orange juice in a saucepan and heat, stirring, until butter is melted and sugar is dissolved. Stir in rum or rum extract. Pour over crêpes and serve immediately.

Yield: 12 to 15 5-inch crêpes.

FRUITED CUSTARD CRÊPES

Custard Sauce:

2 eggs	1⅓ cups milk
¼ cup sugar	1 teaspoon vanilla
Pinch of salt	

Crêpes:

2 cups fresh fruit	2 tablespoons orange
2 tablespoons superfine	liqueur, Kirsch, or
sugar	Cognac (optional)
Juice of ½ lemon	12 dessert crêpes
	¼ cup confectioners' sugar

To prepare custard sauce, place eggs, sugar, salt, and milk in top of a double boiler. Cook over moderate heat, stirring constantly, until mixture thickens slightly.

Do not allow it to boil. Stir in vanilla. Strain custard into a bowl, cover with plastic wrap, and chill.

Cut fruit into ½-inch pieces, leaving small berries whole. Fold in sugar, lemon juice, and optional liqueur, and let stand 1 hour.

Preheat oven to 375° F. Spoon fruit onto one edge of each crêpe and roll up. Place close together, seam side down, in a well-buttered shallow baking dish. Dot surface of crêpes with butter. Place in preheated oven 10 minutes. Sift confectioners' sugar over crêpes and serve immediately. Pass custard sauce separately.

Yield: 12 5-inch crêpes.

BAKED ALMOND DATE CRÊPES

1 cup slivered almonds	3 eggs
½ cup finely chopped dates	¼ cup sugar
	2 cups milk, heated
12 dessert crêpes	1 teaspoon vanilla

Preheat oven to 350° F. Combine almonds and dates. Spoon an equal amount of almond mixture on one edge of each crêpe and roll up. Place close together, seam side down, in a well-buttered shallow baking dish just large enough to hold them. Beat eggs and sugar together with a wire whisk. Gradually add heated milk, stirring constantly. Stir in vanilla. Pour custard over crêpes and bake in preheated oven 30 minutes or until custard is set. Let cool to room temperature before serving.

Yield: 12 5-inch crêpes.

COPENHAGEN CRÊPES

¾ cup strawberry preserves	12 dessert crêpes
	⅓ cup sugar, combined with 2 teaspoons cinnamon
1 cup heavy cream, whipped	

Spoon 1 tablespoon strawberry preserves and 1

tablespoon whipped cream in the center of each crêpe. Fold into pocket shapes and arrange on individual plates. Sprinkle lightly with cinnamon sugar. Pass remaining whipped cream separately.

Yield: 12 5-inch crêpes.

PINEAPPLE CRÊPES

1 package (8 ounces) cream cheese
¼ cup sugar
1½ teaspoons grated lemon rind
½ cup crushed pineapple, very well drained
12 dessert crêpes
1 cup sour cream

Beat cream cheese and sugar until light and fluffy. Stir in ½ teaspoon lemon rind and well-drained pineapple. Spoon an equal amount of filling in the center of each crêpe and fold into pocket shapes. Place on individual serving plates, seam side down. Chill 30 minutes. Serve each crêpe wtih a spoonful of sour cream and sprinkle with remaining lemon rind.

Yield: 12 5-inch crêpes.

HOLIDAY CRÊPES

12 crêpes
¾ cup prepared mince- meat
½ cup plus 2 tablespoons butter, softened
1 cup confectioners' sugar, sifted
2 to 3 teaspoons rum or brandy

Preheat oven to 375° F. Spread each crêpe with 1 tablespoon mincemeat. Fold into triangles and place slightly overlapping in a well-buttered shallow baking dish. Dot crêpes with 2 tablespoons butter. Place in preheated oven for 10 minutes. Meanwhile blend together ½ cup butter, confectioners' sugar, and rum or brandy. Transfer crêpes to individual plates and pass hard sauce separately.

Yield: 12 5-inch crêpes.

DESSERT CRÊPES WITH CHERRY SAUCE

3 eggs, beaten
½ cup milk
½ teaspoon almond extract
½ cup sifted all-purpose flour

1 teaspoon baking powder
1 cup maple blended syrup
1½ cups fresh or drained canned cherries

Combine eggs, milk, and almond extract. Add flour and baking powder. Beat until smooth. To cook crêpes, see "How to Make a Perfect Crêpe." Boil syrup over medium heat for 3 minutes. Remove from heat. Add cherries and cool slightly. Fold crêpes into triangles and place on individual serving plates. Spoon hot cherry sauce over crêpes and serve.

Yield: 12 to 15 5-inch crêpes.

CRÊPES WITH STRAWBERRY SAUCE

12 dessert crêpes
½ cup sugar
½ cup cold water
⅛ teaspoon salt
¼ teaspoon powdered ginger

2 cups sliced strawberries
1 cup heavy cream, whipped with
2 tablespoons sugar

Fold crêpes into triangles and place on heated serving platter. Combine sugar and water in saucepan. Cook, stirring, until sugar dissolves. Boil 3 minutes. Stir in salt, ginger, and strawberries. Cool slightly before spooning over crêpes. Pass whipped cream separately.

Yield: 12 5-inch crêpes.

DANISH CRÊPES

12 dessert crêpes
¾ cup whipped cream cheese
1 package (10 ounces) frozen raspberries in quick-thaw pouch

2 teaspoons cornstarch
4 teaspoons water
¼ cup light corn syrup

With a small spatula, spread each crêpe with 1 tablespoon cream cheese. Fold into triangles and place on individual plates. Drain syrup from raspberries into a small saucepan and heat. Dissolve cornstarch in water and stir into raspberry syrup. Cook, stirring, until slightly thickened and clear. Stir in corn syrup and gently fold in raspberries. Spoon sauce over crêpes and serve immediately.

Yield: 12 5-inch crêpes.

LEMON MERINGUE CRÊPES

3 eggs, beaten	¾ cup sugar
½ cup milk	1 teaspoon cornstarch
½ cup sifted all-purpose flour	½ cup water
	2 eggs, separated
1 teaspoon baking powder	Juice of 1 lemon
3 teaspoons grated lemon rind	

Preheat oven to 400° F. Combine 3 beaten eggs and milk. Add flour, baking powder, and 1 teaspoon lemon rind; beat until smooth. Or combine ingredients in a blender or food processor and blend until smooth. To cook crêpes see "How to Make a Perfect Crêpe." Combine ¼ cup sugar and cornstarch in top of double boiler. Stir in water, 2 egg yolks, lemon juice, and ½ teaspoon lemon rind. Place over simmering water and cook, stirring constantly, until thickened and clear. Keep warm over hot, not boiling water. Beat egg whites until frothy. Gradually add remaining ½ cup sugar and beat until stiff but not dry. Gently fold the egg whites into the yolk mixture. Fold in remaining 2 teaspoons lemon rind. Using a small spatula, lightly spread 1 tablespoon meringue over each crêpe; fold into triangles. Place in 2 or 3 overlapping lines in shallow buttered baking dish. Bake in preheated oven 10 minutes. Serve with Lemon Sauce (see recipe).

Yield: 12 5-inch crêpes.

SOUFFLÉED PECAN CRÊPES

5 eggs, separated
⅔ cup sugar
½ cup finely ground
  pecans
2 tablespoons fine dry
  bread crumbs

⅛ teaspoon salt
16 dessert crêpes
2 tablespoons butter
½ cup confectioners'
  sugar

Preheat oven to 350° F. Beat together egg yolks and sugar until very thick. Fold in pecans and bread crumbs. Beat egg whites and salt until stiff but not dry. Fold into egg-yolk mixture. Spoon an equal amount of soufflé mixture into center of each crêpe and fold into pocket shapes. Place slightly overlapping in a heavily buttered shallow baking dish. Place in preheated oven 10 to 15 minutes. Sift confectioners' sugar over crêpes and serve immediately.

Yield: 16 5-inch crêpes.

CRÊPE A LA FRANCAISE

6 eggs
¼ cup flour
2 tablespoons cold water
  Dash salt

2 tablespoons butter,
  melted
Jam or jelly
Confectioners' sugar

Beat together eggs, flour, water, salt, and butter until smooth. To cook crêpes see "How to Make a Perfect Crêpe." Stack crêpes on a tea towel until all are cooked. Using a small spatula, spread crêpes with jam and fold into triangles. Place on individual heated plates. Sprinkle with confectioners' sugar and serve immediately.

Yield: 16 5-inch crêpes.

SERBIAN SNACK CRÊPES

12 dessert crêpes   ¾ cup sour cream
¾ cup orange marmalade   Confectioners' sugar

Using a small spatula, spread each crêpe with 1 tablespoon marmalade, then 1 tablespoon sour cream. Roll up crêpes and place on individual plates. Sift confectioners' sugar over crêpes before serving.

Yield: 12 5-inch crêpes.

APRICOT NUT CRÊPES

1½ cups apricot   2 tablespoons butter
   preserves   1 cup heavy cream
½ cup finely chopped   3 tablespoons confec-
   pecans   tioners' sugar, sifted
15 to 18 dessert crêpes   Grated rind of 1 orange

Preheat oven to 375° F. Combine apricot preserves and pecans. Using a small spatula, spread each crêpe with an equal amount of apricot filling and fold into triangles. Place crêpes slightly overlapping in a well-buttered shallow baking dish. Dot surface of crêpes with butter. Place in preheated oven 10 minutes. Meanwhile beat cream until almost stiff. Add sugar and orange rind and continue beating until stiff. Transfer crêpes to individual plates and pass whipped cream separately.

Yield: 15 to 18 5-inch crêpes.

FLAMBÉED PEACH CRÊPES

2½ cups thinly sliced   2 tablespoons light
   peaches   cream
18 dessert crêpes   2 tablespoons dry sherry
1 cup firmly packed   2 tablespoons Cognac,
   brown sugar   heated
3 tablespoons butter

Spoon peaches into the center of each crêpe and fold

into pocket shapes. Set aside. Combine sugar, butter, and cream in a chafing dish. Heat, stirring occasionally, until butter is melted and sugar is dissolved. Stir in sherry. Add filled crêpes and baste with sauce. Heat Cognac, ignite it, and pour flames over crêpes. Serve immediately.

Yield: 18 5-inch crêpes.

STRAWBERRY CHEESE CRÊPES

1 package (3 ounces) cream cheese	1 cup crushed strawberries
⅓ cup small-curd cottage cheese	12 dessert crêpes
3 tablespoons sugar	¾ cup sour cream
Grated rind of 1 lemon	12 whole, perfect strawberries

Beat cream cheese until light and fluffy. Beat in cottage cheese, sugar, and lemon rind. Fold in strawberries. Spoon an equal amount of filling in the center of each crêpe and fold into pocket shapes. Chill 30 minutes. Arrange crêpes on individual plates and top each with a tablespoon of sour cream and a strawberry.

Yield: 12 5-inch crêpes.

COTTAGE CHEESE CRÊPES

1½ cups creamed cottage cheese	½ teaspoon vanilla
1 egg, lightly beaten	12 dessert crêpes
½ cup sugar	4 tablespoons butter
1 tablespoon flour	1½ teaspoons cinnamon
¼ teaspoon salt	¾ cup sour cream

Combine cottage cheese, egg, ¼ cup sugar, flour, salt, and vanilla and mix thoroughly. Spoon an equal amount of filling in the center of each crêpe and fold into pocket shapes. Melt butter in a skillet. Fry crêpes, a few at a time, folded side down, 1 minute. Turn and fry 1 minute more. Keep warm on a heated serving plate. Continue until all crêpes are done. Combine remaining sugar and cinnamon. Sprinkle cinnamon sugar over crêpes and top each with a spoonful of sour cream.

Yield: 12 5-inch crêpes.

AUSTRIAN CHEESE CRÊPES

¼ cup butter
¾ cup sugar
½ teaspoon vanilla
1 teaspoon grated
   lemon rind
⅛ teaspoon salt
4 eggs

1 cup creamed cottage
   cheese
¾ cup raisins
1½ cups light cream
12 to 15 dessert crêpes
¼ cup chopped walnuts

Preheat oven to 350° F. Cream together butter and ¼ cup sugar. Beat in vanilla, lemon rind, salt and 1 egg. Stir in cottage cheese and raisins. Spoon an equal amount of filling in the center of each crêpe and fold into pocket shapes. Place slightly overlapping in shallow buttered baking dish. Beat together the remaining ½ cup sugar, 3 eggs and light cream; pour over crêpes. Sprinkle with walnuts. Bake in preheated oven 30 minutes, until custard is set.

Yield: 12 to 15 5-inch crêpes.

SCANDINAVIAN DESSERT CRÊPES

3 eggs, beaten
½ cup milk
½ cup sifted all-purpose
   flour
1 teaspoon baking
   powder

¼ teaspoon nutmeg or
   mace
1 cup sour cream
2 tablespoons sifted light
   brown sugar
1 teaspoon grated orange
   rind

Combine eggs and milk. Add flour, baking powder, and nutmeg. Beat until smooth. Or combine ingredients in a blender or food processor and blend until smooth.

To cook crêpes see "How to Make a Perfect Crêpe." Fold crêpes into triangles and place on individual heated serving plates. Combine sour cream, sugar, and orange rind, and top each crêpe with a spoonful of the mixture.

Yield: 12 5-inch crêpes.

GRAND MARNIER CRÊPES

18 dessert crêpes	½ cup orange juice
¾ cup butter	Grated rind of 1 orange
⅓ cup sugar	½ cup Grand Marnier

Fold crêpes into triangles and set aside. Place butter, sugar, and orange juice in a chafing dish. Heat, stirring, until butter is melted and sugar is dissolved. Stir in grated orange rind. Place crêpes in chafing dish and baste with sauce. Heat Grand Marnier, ignite, and pour flames over crêpes. Serve immediately.

Yield: 18 5-inch crêpes.

FLAMING FRUITED CRÊPES

2½ cups orange sections	½ cup water
15 to 18 crêpes	Juice of ½ lemon
¼ cup sugar	⅓ cup apricot brandy
	2 tablespoons Cognac

Spoon orange sections into the center of each crêpe and fold into pocket shapes. Set aside. Combine sugar, water, and lemon juice in a chafing dish. Heat, stirring, until mixture comes to a simmer. Stir in apricot brandy. Add crêpes, seam side down, and baste with sauce. Heat Cognac, ignite, and pour flames over crêpes. Serve immediately.

Yield: 15 to 18 5-inch crêpes.

ISLAND CRÊPES

15 to 18 dessert crêpes
2 tablespoons butter
½ cup white corn syrup
¼ cup water
3 tablespoons Cognac

2 tablespoons coffee
liqueur
½ pint vanilla or coffee
ice cream

Fold crêpes into triangles and place slightly overlapping in chafing dish. Melt butter in saucepan; add corn syrup, water and 1 tablespoon Cognac. Heat and pour over crêpes. Quickly top each crêpe with a small spoonful of ice cream. Heat remaining Cognac, ignite, and pour flames over crêpes. Serve immediately.

Yield: 15 to 18 5-inch crêpes.

CRÊPES FLAMBÉ

12 dessert crêpes
1 can (8 ounces) fruit
cocktail
2 tablespoons sugar
1 teaspoon cornstarch

2 tablespoons water
1 tablespoon Chartreuse
or any fruit-flavored
brandy
2 tablespoons vodka

Fold crêpes into triangles and reserve. Drain syrup from fruit into a chafing dish. Set fruit aside. Stir sugar into syrup and bring to a simmer. Blend together cornstarch and water; add to syrup. Heat, stirring, until mixture is slightly thickened and clear. Stir in Chartreuse and reserved fruit. Add crêpes and baste with sauce. Heat vodka, ignite, and pour flames over crêpes. Serve immediately.

Yield: 12 5-inch crêpes.

CRUZ BAY CRÊPES

2½ cups thinly sliced
   bananas
16 to 18 dessert crêpes
1 cup firmly packed
   brown sugar

3 tablespoons butter
¼ cup water
¼ cup dark rum
Whipped cream

Spoon bananas into the center of each crêpe and fold into pocket shapes. Set aside while preparing sauce. Combine sugar, butter, and water in a chafing dish. Heat, stirring, until sugar is dissolved. Place crêpes seam side down in chafing dish and baste with sauce. Heat the rum, ignite it, and pour flames over crêpes. When flames subside, transfer to individual plates. Pass whipped cream separately.

Yield: 16 to 18 5-inch crêpes.

DESSERT CRÊPES ST. JOHN

3 eggs, beaten
½ cup milk
½ cup sifted all-purpose
   flour
1 teaspoon baking
   powder
¼ teaspoon nutmeg or
   mace
Confectioners' sugar,
   sifted

Lemon juice
2 or 3 firm ripe bananas,
   peeled and thinly sliced
½ cup butter, softened
1 cup confectioners'
   sugar, sifted
2 to 3 teaspoons rum or
   brandy

Combine eggs and milk. Add flour, baking powder, and nutmeg. Beat until smooth. Or combine ingredients in a blender or food processor and blend until smooth. To cook crêpes see "How to Make a Perfect Crêpe." Place 2 crêpes on each serving plate; sprinkle with confectioners' sugar and lemon juice. Divide banana slices among the crêpes. Top with another crêpe and sprinkle with confectioners' sugar. Blend together butter, 1 cup confectioners' sugar, and rum or brandy. Pass hard sauce separately.

Yield: 4 servings.

GENEVA CRÊPES

1 cup raspberry jam
½ cup finely chopped
   almonds
2 tablespoons Cognac

12 dessert crêpes
Confectioners' sugar
½ pint heavy cream,
   whipped

Preheat oven to 375° F. Combine jam, almonds, and Cognac. Spread an equal amount of filling over entire surface of each crêpe using small spatula. Fold crêpes into triangles. Place in two or three overlapping lines in well-buttered shallow baking dish. Bake in preheated oven 15 minutes. Sprinkle with sugar and serve immediately. Pass whipped cream separately.

Yield: 12 5-inch crêpes.

COGNAC CRÊPES

Juice and grated rind
   of 2 oranges
Juice and grated rind
   of 1 lemon
6 tablespoons sugar

6 tablespoons butter,
   preferably unsalted
18 dessert crêpes
¼ cup Cognac

Place the fruit juices and rinds, sugar, and butter in a chafing dish. Stir over low heat until butter is melted and sugar is dissolved. Place one crêpe in the pan, inside facing up, and, using tongs, fold into a triangle. Push crêpe over to the side. Continue until all crêpes are folded. Heat Cognac, ignite, and pour flames over crêpes. When flames have died out, serve the crêpes immediately.

Yield: 18 5-inch crêpes.

CRÊPES SUZETTE

18 dessert crêpes
6 sugar cubes
1 orange
1 lemon
½ cup orange juice
1 cup sweet butter

¼ cup confectioners' sugar
2 tablespoons Cointreau
2 tablespoons Curaçao
2 tablespoons Benedictine
¼ cup Grand Marnier
¼ cup warm Cognac

Fold each crêpe into a triangle and set aside. Rub sugar cubes over orange and lemon rinds until sugar is permeated with oil from the rinds. Add sugar cubes to orange juice. Melt butter in chafing dish. Add orange juice (with sugar cubes), confectioners' sugar, Cointreau, Curaçao, and Benedictine; heat. Add crêpes, one at a time, and turn each crêpe in sauce. Arrange crêpes in overlapping lines in chafing dish. Heat Grand Marnier and Cognac. Ignite and pour flames over crêpes. Serve immediately.

Yield: 18 5-inch crêpes.

VII

SAUCES AND TOPPINGS

CURRY SAUCE

3 tablespoons butter
2 tablespoons finely
   chopped onion
3 tablespoons flour
2 to 4 teaspoons curry
   powder
½ teaspoon salt

Freshly ground black
   pepper
¼ teaspoon ground
   ginger
½ teaspoon sugar
1½ cups milk
Juice of ½ lemon

Melt butter in saucepan; add onion and cook until tender. Blend in flour and curry powder and cook, stirring, 1 minute. Add salt, pepper, ginger, and sugar. Gradually add milk, stirring constantly, until mixture thickens and comes to a boil. Remove from heat; stir in lemon juice. Serve hot.

Yield: 1 cup sauce.

CURRY EGG SAUCE

3 tablespoons butter	½ teaspoon salt
¾ cup finely chopped mushrooms	Freshly ground black pepper
3 tablespoons flour	2 hard-cooked eggs, chopped
2 to 4 teaspoons curry powder	2 tablespoons finely chopped pimiento
1½ cups milk	

Melt butter in saucepan. Add mushrooms and cook, stirring, until liquid given up by mushrooms has evaporated. Add flour and curry powder and cook, stirring, 1 minute. Gradually add milk, stirring constantly, until mixture comes to a boil and thickens. Reduce heat and add remaining ingredients. Serve immediately.

Yield: Approximately 2 cups sauce.

ANCHOVY EGG SAUCE

2 tablespoons butter	1 teaspoon anchovy paste
2 tablespoons finely chopped celery	2 hard-cooked eggs, chopped
2 tablespoons flour	1 tablespoon diced pimiento
1 cup milk	

Melt butter in saucepan; add celery and cook until tender. Blend in flour and cook, stirring, 1 minute. Gradually add milk, stirring constantly, until mixture comes to a boil and thickens. Beat in anchovy paste. Add remaining ingredients and stir until heated through. Serve hot.

Yield: Approximately 1¼ cups sauce.

TOMATO SAUCE

2 tablespoons olive oil
⅓ cup chopped onion
1 can (8 ounces) tomato
  sauce
1 can (16 ounces)
  Italian style tomatoes
¾ teaspoon salt
¾ teaspoon dried basil
½ teaspoon dried oregano
1 bay leaf

Heat oil in a saucepan; add onion and cook until tender. Stir in remaining ingredients. Cook over low heat 30 minutes, stirring occasionally. Remove bay leaf. If you would like a smooth tomato sauce, force through a sieve and discard solids. Serve hot.

Yield: Approximately 1½ cups sauce.

SEAFOOD SAUCE

2 tablespoons butter
2 tablespoons flour
1 cup milk
  Freshly ground black
  pepper
½ teaspoon salt
1 teaspoon lemon juice
½ teaspoon
  Worcestershire sauce
1 cup flaked cooked
  lobster or crab meat
1 tablespoon diced
  pimiento

Melt butter in saucepan; blend in flour and cook, stirring, 1 minute. Gradually add milk, stirring constantly, until mixture comes to a boil and thickens. Add remaining ingredients and stir until heated through. Serve hot.

Yield: Approximately 1½ cups sauce.

BECHAMEL SAUCE

3 tablespoons butter
1 tablespoon finely
   chopped onion
3 tablespoons flour
1 cup chicken broth
½ cup milk
½ teaspoon salt
   Freshly ground
   black pepper
⅛ teaspoon dried thyme

Melt butter in saucepan; add onion and cook until tender. Blend in flour and cook, stirring, 1 minute. Gradually add chicken broth and milk, stirring constantly, until mixture comes to a boil and thickens. Season with salt, pepper, and thyme.

Yield: 1½ cups sauce.

WHITE SAUCE

3 tablespoons butter
3 tablespoons flour
1½ cups milk
½ teaspoon salt
⅛ teaspoon white pepper

Melt butter in saucepan; blend in flour and cook, stirring, 1 minute. Gradually add milk, stirring constantly, until mixture comes to a boil and thickens. Season with salt and pepper.

Yield: 1½ cups sauce.

MORNAY SAUCE

1 recipe White Sauce or
   Bechamel Sauce
¼ cup heavy cream
⅓ cup grated Swiss cheese
2 tablespoons grated
   Parmesan cheese
Pinch of nutmeg

To prepare sauce, combine White Sauce or Béchamel Sauce with heavy cream. Heat, stirring, until sauce comes to a simmer. Lower heat and simmer 10 minutes. Add remaining ingredients and stir until cheese melts.

Yield: Approximately 1¾ cups sauce.

CUCUMBER SAUCE

½ cucumber
1 teaspoon salt
1 cup sour cream or
   yogurt
3 tablespoons finely
   chopped dill pickle

1 tablespoon finely
   chopped scallion
Freshly ground
   black pepper

Cut cucumber in half; remove and discard seeds. Chop unpeeled cucumber into ¼-inch pieces, sprinkle with salt, and set aside 30 minutes. Drain off accumulated liquid. Combine with remaining ingredients and chill 20 to 30 minutes. This must be served soon after preparation.

Yield: Approximately 1½ cups sauce.

LEMON SAUCE FOR ENTRÉE CRÊPES

3 tablespoons butter
3 tablespoons flour
1¼ cups chicken broth
¼ cup lemon juice
   Grated rind of
   1 lemon

Few drops Tabasco
¼ teaspoon salt
Freshly ground
   black pepper

Melt butter in saucepan. Add flour and cook, stirring, 1 minute. Gradually add broth and lemon juice, stirring constantly, until sauce comes to a boil and thickens. Stir in remaining ingredients.

Note: This sauce is excellent with chicken- or turkey-filled crêpes. To use it with fish or seafood crêpes, substitute clam juice for the chicken broth.

Yield: 1¼ cups sauce.

LEMON CHIVE SAUCE

¾ cup grated cucumber
1 teaspoon salt
1 cup chilled mayonnaise
3 tablespoons lemon
  juice

2 tablespoons snipped
  chives
1 teaspoon prepared
  mustard
¼ teaspoon Tabasco

Sprinkle cucumber with salt and set aside 30 minutes. Drain off all accumulated liquid. Combine with remaining ingredients. Chill 20 to 30 minutes before serving. This must be served soon after preparation.

Yield: 1½ cups sauce.

HERB BUTTER TOPPING

1 cup butter
2 teaspoons lemon juice
2 tablespoons finely
  chopped parsley
1 teaspoon thyme,
  tarragon, basil or
  marjoram

1 clove garlic, crushed
  (optional)
Salt and freshly
  ground pepper

Beat butter until light and fluffy. Beat in remaining ingredients until throughly combined. Season to taste with salt and pepper.

Yield: Approximately 1 cup topping.

CURRIED BUTTER

1 cup butter
3 tablespoons sharp
  mustard

½ teaspoon curry powder

Beat butter until light and fluffy. Beat in mustard and curry powder until thoroughly combined.

Yield: Approximately 1 cup topping.

HORSERADISH MUSTARD SAUCE

¼ cup prepared
  horseradish
¼ cup mayonnaise
1 teaspoon prepared
  mustard

1 cup sour cream
2 tablespoons chopped
  parsley

Blend together horseradish, mayonnaise, and mustard; stir in remaining ingredients. Serve very cold.

Note: A good do-ahead sauce that keeps 5 to 7 days in the refrigerator.

Yield: Approximately 1½ cups sauce.

SALMON NEWBURG SAUCE

3 egg yolks, slightly
  beaten
1 cup heavy cream
½ teaspoon salt
¼ teaspoon Tabasco

1 can (8 ounces)
  salmon, drained and
  flaked
2 tablespoons sherry

Combine egg yolks, cream, and salt in top of double boiler. Cook over simmering water until thickened, stirring constantly. Stir in Tabasco, salmon and sherry. Keep warm over hot, not simmering, water, stirring constantly until ready to serve.

Yield: Approximately 3 cups sauce.

VEGETABLE SAUCE

2 tablespoons butter
2 teaspoons finely
  chopped onion
2 tablespoons flour
½ teaspoon salt
  Freshly ground
  black pepper

¼ teaspoon dried
  tarragon
½ cup chicken broth
½ cup milk
½ cup mixed cooked
  vegetables

Melt butter in saucepan; add onion and cook until

tender. Blend in flour and cook, stirring, 1 minute. Gradually add chicken broth and milk, stirring constantly, until mixture comes to a boil and thickens. Season with salt, pepper, and tarragon. Add vegetables and stir until heated through.

Yield: 1½ cups sauce.

MELBA SAUCE

1 package (10 ounces)   1 tablespoon cornstarch
    frozen raspberries,   3 tablespoons water
    thawed but not drained   1 cup sliced peaches
¼ cup currant jelly

Purêe raspberries in blender of food processor and force through sieve to remove seeds. Place raspberry purêe and jelly in saucepan. Blend together cornstarch and water; stir into raspberry mixture. Cook, stirring constantly, until mixture is thickened and clear. Remove from heat; stir in peach slices. Serve warm.

Note: A good do-ahead sauce that keeps well in the refrigerator.

Yield: Approximately 2½ cups sauce.

CHANTILLY TOPPING

1 cup heavy cream   ½ cup sour cream
2 tablespoons honey

Whip cream until almost stiff. Add honey in a thin stream and continue to whip until stiff. Fold in sour cream. Chill, covered, before serving.

Note: This sauce can be made ½ to 1 hour ahead; it does not keep well for a longer period.

Yield: Approximately 2½ cups topping.

BRANDIED FRUIT SAUCE

3 brandied peaches,
   sliced
3 brandied apricots,
   sliced
8 brandied cherries,
   pitted

¼ cup white corn syrup
2 tablespoons Curaçao
   or other white-spirit
   brandy
⅓ cup Cognac

Combine peaches, apricots, cherries, and corn syrup in saucepan; heat to serving temperature. Stir in Curaçao. Heat Cognac, ignite and pour flames over fruit. Spoon sauce over crêpes and serve.

Yield: Approximately 2 cups sauce.

CARAMEL SAUCE

¾ cup firmly packed
   brown sugar
2 tablespoons softened
   butter or margarine

½ cup heavy cream, heated
¼ teaspoon salt

Place all ingredients in blender container. Cover and blend at medium speed until sugar is dissolved. Serve immediately or refrigerate until ready to use. To reheat, stir constantly over a low flame until sauce is hot.

Yield: Approximately 1¼ cups sauce.

COFFEE TOPPING

¼ cup softened butter
½ cup firmly packed
   brown sugar

3 cups confectioners'
   sugar
¼ cup strong cold coffee

Beat together butter and brown sugar until light and fluffy. Add confectioners' sugar and coffee alternately, beating constantly. Chill to the consistency of hard sauce before serving.

Note: A good do-ahead topping that stores well in the refrigerator.

Yield: Approximately 2 cups topping.

HOT FUDGE SAUCE

6 tablespoons butter
2 cups sifted confec-
    tioners' sugar

⅔ cup cocoa
1 cup evaporated milk

Melt butter in saucepan. Add sugar and cocoa and mix well. Gradually add milk and cook, stirring constantly, until mixture comes to a boil. Cook about 5 minutes over low heat, stirring constantly. Serve immediately; or store in refrigerator until ready to use. Reheat over low heat, stirring constantly, until sauce is hot.

Yield: 2 cups sauce.

CHOCOLATE SAUCE

2 teaspoons butter
1 6-ounce package semi-
    sweet chocolate morsels

1 cup evaporated milk

Combine all ingredients in saucepan. Place over very low heat, stirring constantly until chocolate melts. Serve immediately; or refrigerate until ready to use. Reheat over low heat, stirring constantly, until sauce is hot.

Yield: Approximately 1½ cups sauce.

PINEAPPLE RUM SAUCE

1 can (8½ ounces)   3 tablespoons water
  crushed pineapple   2 tablespoons rum
1 tablespoon cornstarch

Place pineapple with its syrup in saucepan. Blend together cornstarch and water; stir into pineapple. Cook, stirring constantly, until mixture is thickened and clear. Remove from heat; stir in rum. Serve immediately.

Note: This is not a do-ahead sauce or a good keeping sauce. It should be used soon after preparation.

Yield: Approximately 1¼ cups sauce.

MAPLE APPLE SAUCE

1 jar (16 ounces)   ¼ cup butter
  applesauce   Grated rind of 1 orange
½ cup maple syrup

Combine applesauce, maple syrup and butter in saucepan; heat, stirring constantly, until hot. Remove from heat; stir in orange rind. Serve warm.

Note: A good do-ahead sauce that keeps well in the refrigerator.

Yield: Approximately 2 cups sauce.

SPIKED APPLESAUCE

1 jar (16 ounces) apple-   ½ teaspoon cinnamon
  sauce   ¼ teaspoon nutmeg
2 tablespoons brown   ¼ cup applejack or
  sugar   Calvados

Combine applesauce, sugar, cinnamon and nutmeg

in saucepan. Place over low heat, stirring frequently, until hot. Stir in applejack. Serve warm or cold.

Note: A good do-ahead sauce that keeps well in the refrigerator.

Yield: Approximately 2 cups sauce.

PEACH SAUCE

1 can (8 ounces)
peach slices
¼ cup sugar
Grated rind of 1 orange
Grated rind of 1 lemon
2 teaspoons cornstarch
3 tablespoons water
2 tablespoons dark rum

Place peaches with their syrup, sugar, and orange and lemon rinds in saucepan. Blend together cornstarch and water; stir into peaches. Cook, stirring constantly, until mixture is thickened and clear. Stir in rum. Serve hot or cold.

Note: A good do-ahead sauce that keeps well in the refrigerator.

Yield: Approximately 1¼ cups sauce.

CHERRY JUBILEE SAUCE

1 can (20 ounces) pitted
Bing cherries
1 tablespoon cornstarch
2 tablespoons sugar
⅛ teaspoon salt
1 tablespoon lemon juice
¼ teaspoon almond extract
2 tablespoons Grand
Marnier, optional

Drain cherries; reserve syrup. Combine cornstarch, sugar and salt in saucepan; stir in cherry syrup. Cook, stirring constantly, until thickened and clear. Remove from heat; stir in cherries and remaining ingredients. Serve hot.

Note: A good do-ahead sauce that keeps well in the refrigerator.

Yield: Approximately 2¼ cups sauce

ORANGE HONEY TOPPING

½ cup softened butter
2 tablespoons honey

2 tablespoons frozen orange juice concentrate

Beat together butter and honey until light and fluffy. Beat in orange juice concentrate. Chill to consistency of hard sauce before serving.

Note: A good do-ahead topping that stores well in the refrigerator.

Yield: Approximately ¾ cup topping

LEMON SAUCE

½ cup sugar
2 tablespoons cornstarch
⅛ teaspoon salt
1 cup water

2 tablespoons butter
½ teaspoon grated lemon rind
¼ cup lemon juice

Blend together sugar, cornstarch and salt in saucepan; stir in water. Cook, stirring constantly, until mixture is thickened and clear. Remove from heat; stir in remaining ingredients. Serve warm.

Note: This sauce should be used soon after preparation.

Yield: Approximately 1¼ cups sauce.

STRAWBERRY SAUCE

2 cups strawberries,   ¼ cup sugar
  halved   3 tablespoons Grand
                                       Marnier

Place strawberries in bowl and sprinkle with sugar. Let stand at room temperature 2 hours. Place strawberries and Grand Marnier in blender or food processor. Turn machine on and off a few times to break up berries. The sauce should not be a purée. If desired, chill 1 hour before serving.

Yield: Approximately 2 cups sauce.

INDEX